Building Positive Relationships with Parents of Young Children

Positive relationships between practitioners and parents are essential for young children's wellbeing, but achieving this can be difficult if there is not enough understanding about how relationships work when one person (the practitioner or teacher) has to play the professional role. Strong communication skills are fundamental to this relationship and to building a sense of community between home and nursery or school.

This new book explores how practitioners can build warm, friendly and caring relationships with parents. It clearly explains the dynamics of a conversation, the theory behind how relationships are formed or destroyed and provides practical strategies to put this knowledge into practice.

Grounded in the theories of attachment, transactional analysis and solution-focused therapy this book will help you to:

- increase your level of self awareness
- improve your listening skills
- understand 'how' to communicate with different parent 'types'
- learn how to conduct an individual parent interview
- develop professional care-giving skills.

Full of practical examples and strategies, this text will be welcomed by Early Years practitioners and students who wish to develop the skills and confidence they need to effectively communicate with the parents of the children they care for.

Anita M. Hughes is a Chartered Educational Psychologist, who has worked with families for over thirty years both for social services (in Early Years) and then in education services before becoming an Independent Consultant and Therapist. She is the mother of two grown-up children.

Veronica Read is a Group Analyst and Independent Educational Consultant. She writes and delivers workshops on attachment for Early Years practitioners and works as a Specialist Teacher for an LEA. She has extensive experience of working with children with social, emotional and behavioural difficulties. Veronica is also a mother of two grown-up children.

Building Positive Relationships with Parents of Young Children

A guide to effective communication

Anita M. Hughes
and
Veronica Read

Routledge
Taylor & Francis Group

LONDON AND NEW YORK

First published 2012
by Routledge
2 Park Square, Milton Park, Abingdon, Oxon OX14 4RN

Simultaneously published in the USA and Canada
by Routledge
711 Third Avenue, New York, NY 10017

Routledge is an imprint of the Taylor & Francis Group, an informa business

British Library Cataloguing in Publication Data
A catalogue record for this book is available from the British Library

Library of Congress Cataloging in Publication Data
Hughes, Anita M.
Building positive relationships with parents of young children : a guide to effective communication / Anita Hughes and Veronica Read.
p. cm.
Includes bibliographical references.
1. Nursery schools--Great Britain. 2. Preschool teachers--In-service training--Great Britain. 3. Parent-teacher relationships--Great Britain. I. Read, Veronica. II. Title.
LB1140.25.G7H85 2011
371.19'2--dc23
2011040682

ISBN: 978-0-415-67956-5 (hbk)
ISBN: 978-0-415-67957-2 (pbk)
ISBN: 978-0-203-80637-1 (ebk)

Typeset in Bembo and Frutiger
by Saxon Graphics Ltd, Derby

Printed and bound in Great Britain by
TJ International Ltd, Padstow, Cornwall

To Ewa, Libby and Beckie

Contents

Figures

Acknowledgements

As authors, our aim has been to write a seamless text. In the few places where a personal voice describes an individual experience, the speaker is Anita M. Hughes in the earlier chapters and Veronica Read in the later ones.

In approaching the theme of this book we have drawn upon the assistance of parents, children and practitioners. For helping to create the enthusiasm for the book and for being willing to share so much, we wish particularly to thank the participants of our workshops of the past few years.

For their resilience and good humour in the face of so much Public Sector change, we wish to thank our specialist teaching colleagues. They work tirelessly to engage parents in their children's learning, demonstrating that listening to parents' voices promotes depth of thinking, intimate care and effective practice.

We owe special thanks to the following people who have been a part of this writing journey: Ewa Gottesman, Kirsty Stickley, Michelle Dows-Miller, Michael Howlett, Pam Millard, Jeanette Walker, Claire Bullen, Cathy Bollom, Libby Caulfield, Peter Danby, Sarah Rozenthuler, Andrew Woodgate, Chrissie Astell and Jacqui Newman.

Foreword

This book is being published at just the right time! Firstly, the Early Years Foundation Stage is being reviewed with a renewed emphasis on parents being asked to be more involved in their child's learning and development as well as more engaged in governance in their settings and schools so as to improve achievement levels for children. Secondly, the 'Key Persons Approach is now well documented as an important backbone to the body of professional work that enables children's well being, learning and equality in the early years. In this way of working it is essential to make close emotional relationships with a child's family as well as with the child. Though practitioners may have had training to work with young children too often effective communication with parents has been a superficial part of initial training or ongoing professional development. Thirdly, as I know in my own family, caring for my elderly parents or my young grandsons, as well as in my professional work of mentoring and training people who work with young children, relationships of love and affection are demanding. Whether empathising with the pain and frustrations of the elderly – or sharing in the exuberances and disappointments of little ones it is tiring, sometimes stressful, often joyful. Those of you who live and love day by day with young children and families need all the support and guidance you can get to manage these stresses and cycles of emotional energy and involvement with each new child and his or her parents... so read on!!

The authors of this book offer practical advice in the context of theory, research, changes and developments over the last 60 years. Social and personal competencies are learnt and built up over time. If we are to enhance our ability to communicate with parents this cannot only be left to chance and personal style. We all need self awareness, strategies and guidance in developing relationships with a key group of children and their families – families similar to our own as well as families from different social and cultural backgrounds. Some families may be facing similar stresses and circumstances to ones we have faced in our own lives as well as challenges and experiences outside our own experiences. This book counsels us to 'walk in another's shoes' and to practice the art of empathy, really listening to parent's and holding a space in our minds to think about what we observe and hear. This advice may sound familiar but the authors' practical style, all the examples from their personal and professional lives and their rigorous references to contemporary knowledge and historical theories opens up new ways of building and mending communications with parents. The accessible style and carefully blocked text and subheadings demystify what some practitioners may have shied away from in the past as an approach that is 'too touchy feely'. Here the authors are forthright at talking about emotions in the professional context of working with young children and we are given the language and understanding to be able to listen to our own and others emotional energies and responses of love and fear and to use those insights for professional dialogue to inform practical actions in what we say and do with parents.

Relationships are hard work, this guidance may be treated like a friend and mentor to take you into the excitements of new relationships with parents and young children, through the dark caves of misunderstandings, out of your comfort zones through the swish, swash, splash of new encounters of communication and partnership and bravely and boldly onwards to a safer place where we nurture and support young children's learning in authentic involvements with their parents. This book is ultimately a tool facilitating effective communication towards 'better outcomes and achievements' for each unique child.

(My adventure metaphor may ring a bell with a story by David Axtell that will be familiar to most Early Years practitioners!)

Dorothy Y. Selleck,
Early Years Consultant

Introduction

We wanted to write this book for three reasons. The first is to raise the status of those working in the field of Early Years. The second is to encourage your confidence and self-belief in the highly important work that you do. The third is to equip you with the understanding and skills to enjoy your relationships with the parents of the children you work with.

We believe that those of you who work in this field, whether as teachers, practitioners, childminders, advisers or whatever your title, are carrying out the most important work in our community. Society at large has not yet recognised this fact because we still value commerce above service. Indeed your salaries in no way reflect the level of responsibility you actually have.

In the last decade, with the rapid developments in technology, great advances have been made in the understanding of infant and early childhood development. John Bowlby's theories of the mid twentieth century regarding the importance of early secure attachments have been catapulted into first place as a frame of reference for understanding early development and shaping our nurturing practice. Babies' brains actually need affection and the early interactions between parents, carers and babies have lasting effects, both positive and negative. A wonderful and thoroughly researched book on this subject is written by Sue Gerhardt and entitled *Why Love Matters* (2004).

For decades we had tunnel vision when it came to understanding how children learn and develop because those with influence became completely captivated by psychologists' embrace of the theories of behaviourism. It was Skinner (1938) and his laboratory experiments with animals that sent us down a road of belief that all human behaviour is learned through a process of conditioning. In short, this principle of conditioning was that behaviour is learned by seeking positive reward and avoiding negative consequences. The observations made of rats learning to press levers created a theoretical model that influenced childcare and education for the next sixty years. The terms 'toilet training' and 'toddler taming' both derive from the behaviourist model.

Then in the mid 1990s Daniel Goleman produced a book called *Emotional Intelligence* (1996), which opened up our thinking about learning and intelligence in a whole new way. Goleman became fascinated with how to *bring intelligence into emotion* (p. xii). He demonstrated through research and individual human stories how people with good social skills (emotional intelligence) were far more successful in life than those with simply good intellectual skills (IQ). Goleman was influenced by the work of Howard Gardner, who developed the theory of multiple intelligences (1983). Gardner proposed there were seven key intelligences, the last two of which he called the *Personal Intelligences*. It is these two intelligences that are at the heart of this book. They are Interpersonal Intelligence and Intrapersonal Intelligence.

Interpersonal Intelligence describes your ability to understand the desires, intentions and motivations of other people. In other words it is about how well you can 'read' other people. However, that is not the whole story because an aspect of this intelligence is the ability to use one's awareness to work successfully and co-operatively with others. Components of interpersonal intelligence would include leadership skills (being able to get groups to co-operate), negotiating solutions (being able to prevent or resolve conflicts) and personal connection (being able to show empathy for another).

Someone with good interpersonal skills will always be attractive to others as a person who is charming and makes them feel good. However, unless you also have good intrapersonal skills (see below) this will not be satisfying. You may gain approval and popularity but you will feel 'empty' at the same time.

Intrapersonal Intelligence is about the ability to look inward. It is the capacity to understand and appreciate your own feelings and motivations, such as fear and compassion, and then be able to use this awareness to regulate your expression of these emotions in a way that is beneficial to yourself and those around you.

It means you need to be true to yourself and to understand what kind of person you are. Are you someone who likes to have people around you all the time? Are you someone who prefers to follow rather than lead? Are you someone who likes things to be organised? It is about recognising and then attending to what 'feeds your soul' that is important in intrapersonal intelligence.

Recognising and developing your emotional intelligence alongside using your understanding and appreciation of attachment theory is at the heart of your success and power in your work with young children. Those of you who actually work with babies and young children on a daily basis are having immeasurable impact on the mental and emotional well-being of the next generation. The highly successful surgeons, politicians, teachers, artists, parents, etc. of the future will only be able to do their work with compassion, integrity, sincerity and confidence if they feel secure within themselves. That level of self-confidence comes from the quality of relationships they make in the first few years of life. You are at the front line of these good relationships. What is more, you are increasingly taking on a responsibility for helping parents gain their self-confidence, both with you and in their parental role.

It is of vital importance that you, as practitioners, recognise, celebrate and take responsibility for the extremely significant part you play in the development of young children and their families. All too often we hide behind our greatness and put ourselves down. It is still a cultural taboo to 'blow our own trumpet' as it were, but unless we recognise the influence we have and the positive futures we can create, we are selling not only ourselves short but also the next generation.

Sometimes people imagine that writing a book involves sealing yourself off from the world for long periods of time. In truth, that does happen but then each day as you return to daily life you cannot help but be deeply affected by what is going on in the outside world. In turn, the world goes on to influence at some level what you write. This book has been finished against a background of this summer's London 'riots'. As writers, we have not been unaffected by the torrent of communications in the press and on TV about a possible explanation for what some, especially the young in our society, were intending to communicate by their actions.

> Children grow to fit the spaces we create for them. If it is big they grow tall. If it is small they rebel.
>
> (Chief Rabbi Jonathan Sacks, *The Times*, 12 August 2011)

Even the smallest sleeping babies in your nurseries 'know' about the outside world, about the influence of the EYFS on their tiny lives and whether Ofsted is visiting that day! They feel the changes in their environment, especially in you, and respond to these communications with all the sensitivity of a weather barometer. We are all from the moment we are born influenced by the social, political and cultural aspects of life around us.

We, as writers, have also been influenced by recent political events, and whatever we come to understand about the root causes of what happened, we believe it involves much of what this book is about. Parents grow to fit the spaces we create for them and what positive things come of allowing them to grow tall, but equally what can happen when we do not create good enough spaces:

- Empathy is eroded.
- Resentment and hurt are not addressed.
- One becomes single-minded and loses sight of another's needs.
- Trust in the security of a relationship is not felt.
- Mixed messages are communicated.

Just as society has specifically to engage with the young people on the streets of London now, so does each of us have to recognise, respond to and own the power of all that we communicate to each other. Engaging empathically with parents is at the heart of this book. We feel passionately about this engagement but we also know that being in a professional relationship with parents involves balance; too much thought and we cannot feel, and too much feeling and we cannot think. We urge you to remain in touch with your passion for children which surely brought you into this work and hope this book helps you to think, always remain curious about, and find the energy for, rescuing miscommunications and misunderstandings with their parents.

Something to reflect upon

Our deepest fear is not that we are inadequate.

Our deepest fear is that we are powerful beyond measure.

It is our light, not our darkness that frightens us.

We ask ourselves, 'Who am I to be brilliant, gorgeous, talented, fabulous?'

Actually who are you not to be?

You are a child of God.

Your playing small doesn't serve the world.

There's nothing enlightened about shrinking so that other people won't feel insecure around you.

We are all meant to shine, as children do.

We were born to manifest the glory of God that is within us.

It's not just in some of us; it's in everyone.

And as we let our own light shine, we unconsciously give other people permission to do the same.

As we're liberated from our own fear, our own presence automatically liberates others.

From *A Return to Love* by Marianne Williamson (1996, pp. 190–1)

Spoken by Nelson Mandela in his Inauguration Speech

PART I

Laying the foundations of communication

CHAPTER 1

Working in partnership with parents

There has been a lot written about the importance of working in partnership with parents over the last few years. With the advent of the EYFS (Early Years Foundation Stage, DfES 2007b and 2007d), which became mandatory in September 2008 in all schools and providers in Ofsted-registered settings for children from birth to five, partnership with parents is now a part of the legal framework.

As Jennie Lindon (2009, p. 2) puts it: 'Establishing and maintaining close contact with young children's families is a professional obligation.'

In this short chapter we shall define what we mean by the term 'parents' and consider how parents' involvement in their children's early education has changed over the past few decades. Consideration will also be given regarding professional boundaries and expectations as well as the cultural diversity of families in the UK today.

Who do we mean when we use the term 'parents'?

It is important at the outset of this book to clarify what we mean when we use the term 'parents'. Families have changed so much in the last thirty years that young children are not necessarily being brought up and cared for just by their birth parents. In the Guidance to the Standards for the Award of Early Years Professional Status (Children's Workforce Development Council (CWDC) 2008) the definition of parents includes 'Mothers, fathers, legal guardians and primary carers of looked-after children' (CWDC 2008, p. 78).

Ute Ward (2009, p. 2) writes:

> The Guidance continues to point out that there may also be other significant adults in a child's life such as a grandparent, an aunt or a new partner of the child's mother. These adults may spend a lot of time with a child, develop loving and supportive relationships with him and are generally seen as being responsible for him. They may also be your main contact with the child's family and be able to tell you much about the child's home environment. In legal terms, however, this does not mean they have parental responsibility.

In this book, when we refer to the term 'parents' we are including not only parents or legal guardians, but all significant adults in a child's life. It may be, for example, that you get to know a child's grandmother far better than his mother because she is the person who mainly brings the child to your setting and fetches him there later in the day.

This book is aimed to help you develop good relationships with all those who care for the children in your setting, which includes significant adults. However, from a legal point of view, only those with legal parental responsibility are allowed to sign consent forms. Those with parental responsibility also need to make a formal agreement with your setting to other adults collecting their child.

How parental involvement in Early Years has changed over sixty years

This book would have had little relevance a few decades ago. Before the 1960s, childcare workers and nursery teachers had little to do with parents as there was the view that the professionals were the experts in children's learning and development and parents should not interfere.

In the 1960s there was more communication but it was rather 'one way'. The professionals used their expertise to inform and educate parents as if they were the only ones who had any knowledge or understanding about children.

In the 1970s childcare workers and teachers became more aware of the value of communicating with parents, but it was limited to the rather narcissistic view of enhancing their own status as professionals with specialised skills and knowledge.

The 1980s was the decade of consumerism, where accountability became the 'buzz' word. Parents now became 'consumers of a service' so the focus of communication was more about meeting the demands and wishes of parents, which meant they were encouraged to discuss policies and procedures and be part of any consultation about their children's welfare and learning.

In the 1990s it became recognised that parents were experts of their own children and they should actively participate in discussions and decision making about their children's experiences in the Early Years settings. Indeed participation was actively requested, especially in pre-school (formally playgroup) and nursery school settings.

In the 2000s the climate changed again. Increasing numbers of mothers working full-time means they have less time and energy to participate actively alongside practitioners. Single parenthood has massively increased from 8% in 1970 to over 25% today (Gerhardt 2010, p. 214) which places extra pressures on those families. Alongside these sociological changes, there have been an increasing number of legal regulations about the roles and responsibilities of professionals, directing and formalising their relationships with parents. This places a requirement on practitioners to have the skills of communication as never before.

What is happening today

In the training courses I have delivered over the past thirty years, I have met and heard the stories of numerous Early Years practitioners describing their relationships with parents. As we enter the second decade of the twenty-first century it seems that it is getting more and more difficult to make and sustain good working relationships.

There are higher expectations from government to 'deliver' a good service (with the 'fear inducing' health and safety restrictions) but there are *confusing messages* about whether we want our children *cared for* and *nurtured* or simply *trained* and *educated*. With the emphasis on 'education' and 'target setting', parents are increasingly 'handing over' their children to the professionals for 'stimulation' or to give parents 'me-time' or time for paid employment, without there being satisfactory acknowledgement of the emotional impact of this 'triangle' of relationships on all concerned. This is discussed in greater detail in Chapter 7 where we read the story of Memhet and his mother.

We also seem to be getting more and more hooked on 'evidence based' information about children's learning, through complicated record keeping. The use of photographs and the Learning Stories (Carr 2001) provide visual or narrative approaches which are certainly attractive. These forms of communication are appealing at lots of levels. They 'tick the boxes' as it were, because the parents get a 'second-hand' glimpse into their child's life in the setting and the practitioners have fulfilled their obligation of keeping parents informed.

However, parents and practitioners alike can become more excited about the *there and then* of what children have *done* rather than the *here and now* of the children's *feelings*. There is not enough conversation about 'delighting' in the children just being who they 'are'. There is also not enough conversation between parents and professionals about 'delighting' in each other. We are sacrificing the importance of relationships by focusing on milestone achievements and how we communicate them.

Being clear about boundaries and core values

The focus of this book is about developing and improving communication skills so we can build better relationships. It is largely about interpersonal relationships and about helping you, the reader, to improve your own self-awareness and confidence. You may find yourself reading and thinking about relationships outside your work. You may find yourself thinking of your other roles in life such as being a partner or spouse, a friend, a sibling, a parent or a grown up child of your own parents. Whilst this will help in your overall personal development and may interest, even fascinate you, it is important to keep in mind, in the context of the purpose of this book, what it means to have a *professional relationship*.

The professional relationship

Whether you are a childminder, manager of a day care nursery, nursery school or pre-school, or a key person for a small group of children in an Early Years setting, you have contracted through a formal agreement (which may or may not directly involve a financial payment) to be responsible for the care and well-being of someone else's child.

This will mean that both you and the parents will have agreed, before the child even starts, on the policies of your setting that underpin good professional practice. It is extremely important to be clear about the boundaries (such as when a child must be picked up by). You need to know and be clear about what is negotiable with parents and what is not. Parents need to be clear about the expectations of the setting and the core values of that setting, to avoid confusion and misunderstanding in the future. It is usually misunderstanding that is underneath all relationship breakdowns. Chapter 9 on 'Dealing with difficulty' will look into this area in more detail.

Cultural diversity

We recognise that in the UK we live in a multi-cultural society. It brings richness to all our experience, not least in our Early Years settings. However, it can also create barriers and conflict if we are insensitive to the unique perspectives or differing communication styles of other cultures.

The ways people deal with feelings, especially disappointment, anxiety, fear, embarrassment and anger, vary considerably. It can sometimes be difficult to discern, for example, if parents are pleased or not with the work you are doing with their child. We all want to feel that our efforts are being acknowledged, but it is important not to jump to conclusions about parents' attitudes, simply from their behaviour. For example, if a parent does not look at you directly, it may be that in that parent's culture sustained eye contact is interpreted as a challenge to authority, whereas we could interpret it as lack of interest.

Be sensitive in the way you communicate

Practitioners need to be sensitive to the different values, experiences and beliefs that may be held by various cultures and ethnic groups.

The best ways to be sensitive are:

- Always express courtesy (as you would a guest in your own home). After all, the parent is bringing her child to 'your' working domain.
- Give parents enough time and the opportunity to express themselves in the way that is comfortable for them. For example, in some cultures, people like to exchange lengthy greetings and pleasantries before they speak about the more formal 'business'. Although you might be feeling rushed it is important to give the parents that time. Not only will you enjoy the relationship more, it will also save you time by avoiding problems in the future.
- Be 'yourself' (your professional and dignified self) with parents, expressing yourself with sincerity. Even if the parents do not speak English very well they will nevertheless 'pick up' how sincere you are in your attempts to make a relationship with them.

- Do not be afraid of asking parents questions about their culture and traditions. If you are genuinely interested and show that you want to be able to incorporate as much of the family's cultural style as is possible, for the child's benefit, then this will enhance the experience for all concerned.
- If you are giving the parent a written message, try to do so in the parent's native language and use an appropriate reading level. (Some parents' literacy skills are very weak.)

When parents are friends, neighbours or employers

It is likely that you may have a relationship outside of work with some parents, especially if you live near the setting in which you work. This can pose difficulties, as the blurring of boundaries between being friendly and being a friend can lead to uncertainties and inappropriate ways of relating.

As Jennie Lindon (2010, p. 13) writes: 'Your professional role means that you have to step back a little and to be very clear in your own mind over the limits to open communication with friends on some topics.'

Ute Ward (2009, p. 96) expresses it well when she says:

> Neighbours relate differently to each other than employee and employer do, the way friends behave varies differently from the way family members interact, and so on. These different relationships, which can exist between the same two people depending on the situation they find themselves in, can lead to a confusion of roles and hence to uncertainty about what constitutes appropriate behaviour.

Acknowledgement is essential

In order to tread the fine line of professional friendliness and friendship it is absolutely essential that your professional role is acknowledged along with the possible confusions and uncertainties. If you do not do this, then there is a strong likelihood there will be conflict and bitterness in the future. It is human nature to try and avoid 'awkward' and difficult 'situations' but you simply cannot do this in your professional role.

Whilst you can choose to avoid a friend, decide not to see a relative that weekend or invite a neighbour into your home, when you are wearing your 'practitioner' hat you have to keep to the 'rules' of professional conduct.

Some common scenarios

- A parent takes on an additional role in your setting. This arouses suspicious feelings from other parents that this person's child may get preferential treatment. There needs to be clarity about the selection process of volunteers or staff and how their skills might be used as well as a statement about volunteers or staff having their own children in the setting.

- You are out with friends (one of whom also happens to be a parent in your setting) and the conversation steers into 'gossip' about one of the families. It is important that you 'opt out' of this conversation by maybe saying, 'I'm afraid I'm going to have to wear my work hat right now and you know that I won't talk about other families like this. I know you will understand.'

- A parent, who is also a friend, is repeatedly late picking up his/her child, giving you excuses that incorporate things like, 'You're my friend and you know how disorganised I can be!' It is important to make it clear that whilst it might not matter in your own home, when you are at work you cannot accept this as it has a negative impact on the child (who is fretful about why his mummy has not turned up when all the other mummies have) and there is a clear picking up time that everyone needs to keep to.

- As this short chapter has revealed, the idea of partnership with parents is both an evolving and a complex process. It also presents with challenges as well as opportunities. However, if we open our eyes to them and develop our awareness and skills to navigate the relationships in a caring and professional way, there are rich treasures to be found for everyone.

CHAPTER 2

What do we mean by communication?

The difference between 'tuning in' and 'communication'

Over the years we have delivered many workshops examining how to communicate more effectively with children, parents and colleagues. A favourite exercise is to divide the group into two halves and invite one half to write all the words that come to mind which they associate with the word *Communication*. The other half of the group does the same but with the words *Tuning In*.

What is fascinating is that a strong pattern always emerges. Words that appear on both lists are usually listening, body language, talking, etc. However on the 'tuning in' list there are usually the phrases 'recognising feelings', 'getting on the other person's wavelength', 'knowing how the other person is feeling'. These kinds of phrases never reach the 'communication' list.

- Communication involves conveying a message.
- Tuning in involves making a relationship.

Tuning in is about communicating with our hearts. If we want to be more effective and successful in the way we communicate with parents, then we must learn how to make positive relationships with those parents. We must learn not only how to 'show' effectively that we care but also to feel genuinely that we care. Caring about someone is different from simply liking or disliking someone. Liking and disliking are judgements we make about someone, but caring is about connecting without judgement. You can care about someone you don't really like if you are able to see the other person as a fellow human being with feelings just like you have. It can be difficult if you are not naturally attracted to someone's personality, but it is possible and necessary if you are working with children as you need to make relationships with their parents.

It takes time and skill to make any positive relationship. Some parents may feel they have neither the time nor the skills to make a positive relationship with you, the 'expert'. This makes it even more important that you, the professional, can develop the confidence and skills to tune in and communicate with parents so that they feel safe and confident with you.

A definition of communication

If you look up the definition of the word *communication* in any dictionary you will find that it describes the word as the act of 'imparting' or 'conveying' information. There is a sense that it is a one-way trip. Indeed, you could say that the *Radio Times* communicates to us what is on television and a railway timetable communicates the train times. A news broadcaster will give us the latest stories of what is happening in the world and a poster may advertise a product such as perfume. These are all forms of communication which give us straightforward factual information. If you ask someone what the time is, you might think you are simply going to receive a factual answer such as whether it is 10 o'clock. However, that is not the case!

The moment there is a 'receiver' in a line of communication, it becomes a two-way trip. There will immediately be an emotional response. There may be some feeling of anticipation about a television programme to be broadcast that evening, or frustration that the train times are not going to work for you. You may feel distress or a sense of helplessness from the images or telling of the latest conflict or natural disaster that has happened on a news broadcast. You may feel a desire to purchase the advertised perfume. However impersonal the 'giver' of communication might be, the receiving end will always involve a personal and emotional response of one kind or another.

When it comes to a personal encounter, something more happens. Let us consider the case of asking someone the time. First of all you might have to engage that person's attention by saying, 'Excuse me, I hope you don't mind me troubling you?' Then that person gives you a response that might be, 'Of course not, how can I help you?' Then a short two-way conversation will ensue until a farewell exchange of thanks and goodbye takes place.

You may now have established what the time is, but what you will have also had is an *emotional experience*. Did you leave that person feeling uplifted by his engaging smile, enthusiasm, warmth and friendliness? Did you walk away feeling ashamed because that person seemed to sneer at you? Did you separate feeling angry and frustrated because that person was impatient and unfriendly? Did you feel rejected because that person did not even respond, but turned his back on you? Did you even notice how that person made you feel? Did you wonder what the other person was feeling or what the other person thought of you?

Communication involves entering into a relationship

Whenever we communicate with someone else we enter into a relationship. The relationship might last only a few moments but it will immediately have an effect on our emotional well-being. I have noticed that when I am driving my car and let someone out of a side turning into the road in front of me, the enthusiastic and appreciative smile and hand gesture of thanks can give me a great feeling for several moments. My experience in shops varies greatly too. I actually enjoy visiting my local post office, where I am known by name, because the friendliness of the people always makes me feel happy even if we are only talking about the weather! However, I can sometimes meet a person at the checkout in a supermarket and get a feeling that I am just a 'no one'. It is a dispiriting feeling. I suspect that is what some of the checkout assistants feel about themselves in that role. We might have hardly any personal exchange at all. For example, 'Put your card in' are the only words spoken by this person who makes no eye contact with me. I leave the supermarket feeling rather flat and often pressurised by the impatience of those waiting to be served after me. I expect this is a familiar experience for everyone.

However, I was struck recently by an encounter I had in the supermarket with one particular cashier whom I had not met before. He had a beaming smile and immediately engaged in friendly conversation about the weather followed by the products he was scanning. He made positive comments about the things I had chosen to buy and asked me my views of others he had not personally tried. In moments I felt that somehow we knew one another; he was another fellow human being like me. We had things in common, even if it was only that we liked the same types of biscuits. It was such a small thing at one level and yet at another it had a significant impact because it made me feel good for the rest of the day and I found myself being more consciously friendly towards other people I met afterwards. I wonder if he had the same effect on all the rest of his customers that day.

Communication is more than simply conveying a message; it's about entering into a relationship.

The influence of technology

The desire and means to communicate with others have never been as great as they are today. We are in an age which, in future generations, will probably be looked back on as 'the era of communication'.

Up until only recently we could communicate face to face, by handwritten or typed letter, through the printed word or by landline telephone. The use of a fax machine was viewed as a great advance. However in the last decade, with the advent of mobile phones and the internet, the opportunities to communicate have exploded into myriad new formats from email to text, Skype to Facebook, Twitter to Google. The technological advances of just the past five years have turned mobile phones into mini computers, where we can find information or communicate with others from wherever we are simply by touching a slim hand-held device that can be carried in a pocket.

Indeed so seductive is the technology that we are using it more and more as a way to communicate with others. Much of the time it is a 'messaging device' (whether in picture or written word format) where the receiver of that information will pick it up at another time, which could be seconds, hours or days later. However, with the easy access to webcams and so on we can now actually have face to face conversations with people who might be halfway across the world. The advances in technology have made it wonderful for people living far away from one another to keep in touch in a very personal way.

However, there are some real dangers with the increasing reliance on technology as a means of communication.

- We are in danger of getting overwhelmed by the sheer volume of information we are receiving and true communication might be compromised.
- Messages in the form of text or pictures are open to misunderstanding and abuse.
- Children and vulnerable adults can get easy access to inappropriate information (such as pornography).
- 'Cyber' bullying is becoming common both in schools and in the workplace.
- A lot of the communication, particularly on email or on mobile phones, becomes vacuous, sterile and empty because it is such repetitive chatter.
- Due to the speed of creating and sending messages, there is less attention towards accuracy and errors are often made.

If we are mindful of the dangers of technology as a means of communicating with others, we can also be aware of, and build on, the benefits. Nurseries up and down the country are creating their own websites, for example. The use of digital cameras catches children learning and having fun for their families to see, share and enjoy. Many of the pictures are printed and stuck up on walls or in albums but others are put on rolling screens at the nursery entrances to create a warm welcome. These are examples of positive uses of technology to communicate with parents. However, the focus of this book will be on building positive and meaningful relationships with parents through becoming a good communicator in your face to face communication with others.

Communication from the heart

The most important thing about being a good communicator is to communicate from the heart. For communication is an art more than a skill and it comes from the heart, from love. A person may have good communication skills but never really be a good communicator because she is only operating from the head.

When I say we need to communicate from the heart I am talking about feelings of compassion for the other person. As I said at the beginning of this chapter, you need to care about the other person even if you don't like him. It might sound like a tall order, but it's not only possible but necessary. The current president of the USA, Barack Obama, did not rise from insignificance to prominence just because he is a good orator; it was because he really cares about the lives of American people. We just know he speaks from the heart. We believe in what he says. He inspires hope. He got to that place because he listened to others with an open heart and an open mind.

This is where you need to begin: with an open heart and an open mind. This book will give you some ideas about how communication works and some ways to improve your skills, but the most important thing is to feel inspired, to be open-hearted with parents and colleagues. The other thing is that when you are with a parent (or anyone for that matter), whether it is for a few moments or for a long conversation, you should treat that person as if she is the most important person in the world. In those moments that you share together, you and she are the most important people in the world to you.

Building relationships of trust

I have so far talked about communication as a two-way exchange that involves information and emotion. However, when you are working with a parent there is an extra dimension in your relationship that makes it very powerful and important. You are by and large talking about that parent's child. Although many of your encounters will be light-hearted, fun, simple and short, each and every one is laying a foundation of trust between you and the parent about a most treasured part of their lives. Some parents find the experience of looking after their young child or children very difficult. The demands of parenthood have proved much more challenging than they could have imagined. All parents get tired and overwhelmed. I know that I did when my children were small, and those of you reading who are parents will know what I am talking about. The way parents hide their feelings of weariness and inadequacy will vary. They may seem not to care, be frivolous or inattentive towards their child when they are with you.

This is where it is really important to build up feelings of trust between you and the parents. If you fail to build up that trust you will find that a parent will become difficult, defensive, avoidant or distant. It is easy to blame a parent when relationships become awkward, but we need to look at the way we have handled things ourselves. Have you paid enough attention to building up that trust? In your training you have probably focused on the importance of developing a trusting and secure relationship with the children. Elinor Goldschmied was adamant that children need to make secure relationships with a key person, when they are cared for outside the family home (Elfer, Goldschmied and Selleck 2011). This is now common practice in most settings these days and is part of the principles and practice of the EYFS. However it is *equally important* to build a secure relationship with the child's parents.

Here are some factors that need to be considered in your communication with parents, which are *particular* to those of you working with young children.

- It is a daily/regular encounter (or as often as the child attends). It is not like a casual encounter with the person serving you in the local supermarket.
- It is about someone's child, who is a living, young, vulnerable human being. It is not about the local pub or the latest film at the cinema.
- It is about building up a trusting relationship that in turn has an impact on the child's attachment experiences with both you and the parents. It is not simply building a one-on-one relationship with another adult as a nurse might do with an adult patient.

It is a professional relationship and, even if you get on very well with a parent, it is important to remember that she is not a friend in the working environment. If a parent of a child is your friend or a relative then you will need to work doubly hard on the boundaries between your professional relationship and your personal relationship and keep them separate. (I will refer to this in more detail a little later.)

The energies of emotion

The whole of the world is made up of energy. There is nothing completely solid or permanent on this earth. Everything is in motion: a mass of tiny molecules whizzing around, invisible to the naked eye. When you look at something like a table, it seems permanent and solid but that is only an illusion. It is when you watch the movement of the sea and the wind that you get the obvious visible signs of energy in motion.

So what about the emotional energy that surrounds us? You only need to enter a room where there is a conversation going on and, even if you can't hear what is actually being said, you can probably pick up on the energy of that exchange. Was it awkward? Was the atmosphere intense, light-hearted or agitated? You can always tell if a party is in full swing or whether it is drawing to an end. What about Christmas? That is always a time of heightened emotional energy, when there can be the extremes of sublime joy, poignant sadness or even downright hostility.

You might be on a train and suddenly you can feel tension in the air as an argument breaks out. Maybe on that same train there are people laughing together and even if you are not part of the conversation you might find yourself smiling. I remember a few years ago that I was on a train travelling from London to Manchester. It was during the early winter and we had not seen snow in years. Suddenly there was a tremendous snowstorm and through the thick flakes flying around we could see the landscape rapidly turning white before our eyes. At first people simply glanced out of the windows; then this was soon followed by a flurry of texting and ringing friends on mobiles. People wanted to share this experience but went beyond the reaches of the train to make those connections. However, the excitement of the carriage became so charged that what had been a quiet atmosphere of passengers dozing and reading turned quite suddenly into spontaneous chatter between strangers and we all felt a sense of togetherness sharing in this experience. For a short while this train of strangers had become a community.

We cannot fail to 'feel' the atmosphere of togetherness and excitement at protest marches and big sporting, musical or festival events. However, something might happen between one or two people and the atmosphere at the same event can change and feel threatening. That threatening 'feel' can quickly spread like wildfire, sometimes generating panic or aggression. The energy has shifted. As Marianne Williamson (1996) states, all energy in communication is about either *love* or *fear*. Even when we are not directly in the company of others, we are picking up on the energies around us. What is more, we are increasingly picking up on the energies of fear and they are contaminating our lives.

TABLE 1 *The two energies in communication*

LOVE	FEAR
Appreciation	Distrust
Trust	Timidity
Gratitude	Anger
Joy and delight	Defensiveness
Forgiveness	Aloofness
Beauty	Narrow-mindedness
Harmony	Ugliness
Tolerance	Disharmony
Compassion	Blame
Confidence	Rejection
Affection	Distress
ENERGISES	PRODUCES STRESS
AND GIVES LIFE MEANING	DISTRESS AND ILLNESS

How the energy of fear is communicated

All around our country there are CCTV cameras in our towns and neighbourhoods. These devices are supposed to give us a feeling of safety, but they usually have the opposite effect. You feel 'watched', which makes you somehow on the defensive, or the presence of cameras may suggest the area is dangerous enough to warrant them, so making you fearful. There is a sense that it does not actually prevent crime, but simply records it when it happens. Indeed the CCTV images of violent crime or the poignant 'last moments' of those who have been murdered that are shown on TV are giving us emotional responses that reverberate within us even if we do not consciously realise it. These are examples of the energies of fear.

Since first writing this chapter there have been the London riots that spread across the country like wildfire (6–9 August 2011). The vivid images of buildings aflame, wanton looting and surges of 'hooded' crowds filled our television screens and leapt into the emotional circuits of our brains. The energies of fear also spread around the world like wildfire.

This is an email extract from a young person who lives in a quiet provincial town about forty miles from London:

> All my friends were calling from London and they just kept saying, 'There's just a weird feeling about the place', and it seemed to spread right up to here. The café

I work in was deserted and everyone was walking down the street with their heads down, completely untrusting – something that is very unusual for this area.

The energies of fear are everywhere. We are worried about climate change, about paedophiles, about health and safety issues, about losing our jobs, about swine flu or superbugs in hospitals, about the fate of those ravaged by war or environmental disaster. We are reminded daily through all the various means of communication of the possibilities of terrible things happening over which we have no control. Is it any wonder that we also have such high levels of stress in our society? Many of the major physical conditions such as heart disease and cancer are triggered by stress. There are increasing numbers of the population (including children) who are being medicated for mental conditions, which are all exacerbated by the negative energies of fear.

Arlo Wally Minto (1994) writes:

> Your brain is a computer-like guidance mechanism and it guides you according to the beliefs you have programmed it with; however there are different degrees of belief . . . The simple truth is that the things we believe in more strongly than anything else are the things that we fear.

Recently a friend from Norway came to visit me for a few days. She had been travelling in the UK and a few days earlier had developed an acute pain in her neck and shoulder, together with sensations of numbness in her hands. She had been coping with the pain using pain killers, but during the first night she stayed with me, she tossed and turned in agony as the pain killers did not work. The next morning she told me about her pain and her distress as she hobbled into the kitchen. What became particularly apparent was that her distress was heightened because she had convinced herself she was about to have a heart attack, and her belief that she might be in a life threatening situation terrified her. She told me that she had been to see a doctor a few days earlier who had been 'vague' and simply recommended she continue with pain killers. She had not been reassured. In fact her fears had only been heightened because he failed to give her a diagnosis. She was desperate to 'get back home' to Norway where she could 'talk' to her own doctor, whom she trusted, and get a diagnosis.

I suggested she visit my local osteopath and in desperation she agreed. We were lucky to secure an appointment within half an hour. At the end of the forty-minute consultation and treatment my friend appeared with a beaming smile. The pain was still there, but it no longer mattered. The osteopath had *listened* to her with *empathy* and *care* and was able to reassure her by explaining what was happening to her body. She did have some manipulation, but the pain began to ease because her fear had eased. Indeed, she said that she was now going to visit an osteopath in Norway and work on being kinder to her body and tune into the little aches and pains a bit more in the future.

If we become focused on the energies of *fear* at the expense of the energies of *love*, then life becomes sad, difficult and painful.

How the energy of love is communicated

So let us consider the energies of love. When the sun shines and it is warm, the whole atmosphere seems to change! Perfect strangers smile and greet one another on the street. Indeed people come outside and enjoy the colours and the vividness of nature. There is a feeling of camaraderie, which you can't quite put your finger on, when you see others out and about on a sunny day.

Have you ever been in hospital or in the company of someone who is dying? The tenderness and love shown by the nursing and caring professions can be stunning, even though what they actually do may look very ordinary and simple. My elderly godmother was dying of cancer last year and was being cared for in the home of her niece. I was privileged to be there when the daily nursing team came to visit. The gentleness and sensitivity those people showed towards this lady, to help her retain her dignity and to minimise her pain and discomfort, brought tears to my eyes. For example, they spoke softly and gently stroked her brow as they talked to her.

Acts of kindness generate energies of love that can ripple out well beyond an initial kind gesture. Indeed kindness is at the heart of compassion and the energy of love.

As I write this, the preparations for the Royal Wedding of Prince William and Kate Middleton are in full swing. You may not be interested in the royal family or may even be anti-royal. However, whatever your views, the event has triggered a whirlwind of positive energy as communities up and down the country are preparing for their 'street' parties and garden barbecues. The energy of love brings people together and creates a sense of interconnectedness. The energy of fear divides people and creates feelings of loss, isolation and desolation.

Touch and the communication of love

Touch is one of the most powerful ways to communicate the energy of love. A friendly handshake on greeting someone communicates connection and a welcome into a relationship. An arm over a shoulder is comforting for someone at times of distress. A gesture of the light touch on someone's hair can communicate warmth in a relationship. Patting someone's knee can communicate, 'I understand, I care and I am here for you.' It can also communicate, 'I agree with you.' A 'high five' (single raised hands clapping together between two people) communicates shared delight. A hug can communicate a warm farewell or greeting. Sometimes you may hug someone spontaneously to communicate you are sharing in his success or delight.

Touch is a wonderful tool for healing. Just think when a child grazes a knee or bangs the head; our response is to kiss it to make it better. We stroke a child's brow who is struggling with fever. The washing of someone's feet is amazingly rejuvenating. Stroking animals like dogs, cats and rabbits is enormously healing for those who are sick, elderly and infirm and has been found to be really helpful for autistic children and adults.

It is a natural thing, all over the world, for people to touch each other as a way of sharing love and care. The manner in which we do this varies from culture to culture, but the desire to make physical contact is present in all of us.

Beware of touch as a communication of fear

For many people, and you may be one of them, touch can feel threatening or intrusive. Although many people describe themselves as being 'touchy feely', there are probably even more people who find touch difficult, and we need to be aware of this and respect it. The way to assess this, if someone does not actually say anything, is to watch the way she greets you or touches her own child for example. If she shakes your hand, you might find she extends her arm further and with the elbow much straighter. This keeps you at a safe distance. That person is likely to let go of your hand within a couple of seconds. However someone who likes touch is likely to have her elbow at her side so that she is standing closer to you and may even shake your hand with both of hers. She is also likely to stand there holding your hand for maybe ten or twenty seconds without even realising it!

Someone who finds touch difficult may allow his own child to hug his leg or tug a piece of his clothing, but does not immediately pick up that child. However, someone who likes touch will actively seek opportunities to stroke, hug or kiss his own child.

What kind of person are you? Are you someone who does not like touch? Then you will understand how touch can feel intrusive or threatening. Are you someone who seeks out physical contact? Then you need to be aware of your own behaviour and sensitive towards others. It is very important to be aware of the kind of person you are so that you can understand others and moderate your own behaviour accordingly.

A pat on the shoulder could be felt as an aggressive push. A handshake greeting may unwittingly communicate formality rather than friendliness. A hug may feel overwhelming and even painful.

You even need to be careful about how close you are to the other person. Instinctively we get close to someone who wants comfort or to share something intimate. However, there are many people and children who are very sensitive about their physical space. It takes time and trust before they will let you show friendliness through physical contact.

In the more daily contact you have with parents and colleagues, be aware of how close they choose to stand near you. Does the parent you are talking to stand close enough so that you could touch her, or is that person just far enough away from you so that if you did reach out you could not quite touch her? You need to respect the space the parents choose, for getting physically close to some parents can feel too intimate or overwhelming and they may avoid talking to you altogether. As you build up trust, then the physical space between you might get a bit less over time. However, there are other parents who might find that you are 'stand-offish' or too formal if they seek close proximity and you stand at a 'non-touching' distance. It is important to notice how parents behaves so that you can 'match' it and help them feel comfortable.

We are currently in an era where touch is much more acceptable and many people like to hug each other as a form or greeting or comfort. What is the acceptable code of conduct in your setting? If there are occasions when a hug is acceptable or seems the right thing to do, it is less threatening to have contact only with the chest and cheek (rather than full body contact). It is also a good idea to hug his left side with the left side of the heads together. In this way the hearts are placed directly over each other and there is an exchange of heart energy (Minto 1994, p. 45). Even those people who find touch difficult appreciate this form of hug as it taps into the energies of love rather than fear.

The taboo of the 'love' word

What about your work? How much do you love your work? How much do you love the children you work with? Love is a word that we are often afraid of using and yet if we ignore it we are in danger of diminishing the magnificence of life. Here is a story which has a lot to tell us about love in the workplace.

The three stonemasons

Once upon a time, many hundreds of years ago, when the great buildings of Europe were being built, the foundations of a magnificent cathedral were being laid in a large town in the centre of the continent.

One of the monks of the town had been given the job of supervising all the labourers and artisans. In order to start this task, he decided he would carry out a study into the working practices of the stonemasons as he could see they were already busy at work cutting the blocks that would form the foundations of the building. He chose to interview three of the stonemasons to find out what they thought of their work and how they were getting on.

He went over to the first stonemason and said, 'My brother, I hope you don't mind if I interrupt your work. I wonder if you could tell me something about what you are doing.'

The first stonemason stopped what he was doing and looked at the monk. He wore an expression of irritation and suspicion on his face. 'Well, what can I say?' responded the stonemason in a roughly spoken grumble. 'You can see what I am doing; it is mindless, soul destroying work. I am sitting in front of this block of stone measuring a metre by half a metre by half a metre and have to chisel away at it day by day. No one will ever see my work as it will be in the foundation of the building, yet I am expected to create a perfect finish. My hands are hard, my body bent, my hair is going grey and I am always exhausted; this work is sending me to the grave'

The monk thanked the first stonemason for talking to him and went on to the second stonemason. 'My brother', he said, 'I hope you don't mind if I interrupt your work. I wonder if you could tell me something about what you are doing.'

'Of course I can', said the second stonemason as he put down his chisel to answer. 'As you can see, I am working on this block of stone measuring one metre by half a metre by half a metre. It's like I am carving out a future for myself because the wages not only feed my family and pay for a roof over my head but my children are getting an education. This work means that my children will have the chance of a better future.'

The monk thanked the second stonemason for talking to him and went on to the third stonemason. At first he almost did not to want to interrupt this man, so deeply absorbed he seemed in his work. However, when he introduced himself as he had done to the other stonemasons, the third stonemason looked up at him with a shining smile and invited him to sit down with him.

'I would be delighted to tell you about my work', said the third stonemason with joy and enthusiasm in his voice. 'I am the luckiest man in the world. Here I am with this block of magnificent stone measuring one metre by half a metre by half a metre. Every day I am working on creating something of beauty that will one day be a small part of this glorious building that will bring spiritual inspiration and joy for generations to come. In my humble way I know that I am part of something that is greater than me, a building that will stand as a beacon to the glory of life and love for each other. Every day I thank God that I am able to be part of this great project.'

The monk thanked the third stonemason for talking to him and went home filled with great energy and a sublime peace. He went to bed and slept peacefully and the next morning he resigned his position as supervisor and apprenticed himself with the third stonemason.

Adapted from *The Magic of Metaphor* by Nick Owen (2001)

You are doing the most valuable work there is

Which of the stonemasons do you identify with? Which of the stonemasons would you want to become like? The salary and status of those working with very young children and their families do not reflect the value of the work you are doing. However, in essence, you are doing the most valuable work there is. For you are key people in the lives of the children you work with. You may never see what kind of adults they will become, but if you can openly give love, guidance and care to those children and parents now, they have a chance to become reliable, confident and caring people in the future.

CHAPTER 3

Listening – the number one communication skill

> The reason why we have two ears and one mouth is that we may listen more and talk less.
>
> (Zend-Avesta, Zoroastrian sacred scripture)

However good our intentions are, our communication skills will not be effective and our relationships will be of limited quality unless we know how to listen. We all remember being told to 'listen' at school and we may even find ourselves being asked by our friends and family to listen to them now, but what does that actually mean? For many people it simply means keeping quiet and giving the other person a chance to have his 'say'. However, this is a very superficial, limited and 'one-way' view of this skill. Listening is an active verb. It involves giving as well as receiving, giving meaning to the message and value to those who are being listened to. It also involves being fully present. If you improve your listening skills this will improve your ability to influence, persuade, negotiate and reassure as well as reduce misunderstandings.

Here are four main reasons to listen:

- We listen to obtain information.
- We listen to learn.
- We listen for enjoyment.
- We listen to understand.

However the most important reason to listen in the context of this book is:

- We listen to make good relationships.

Recently I was with a good friend whom I have known for twenty-five years and she was telling me about the sadness she feels about her friendship with someone she has known since she was a teenager. She has shared important milestones of her life with this friend but she feels that the friendship is over. There have been no arguments, crises or incidents that have triggered my friend's feelings. This is what she told me:

Every time I see my friend Hannah all she seems interested in doing is talking about herself and her family. Whenever I say anything to her about my life she just stares at me without smiling. She doesn't even move. It's rather creepy. She never asks me anything and it's like she's just waiting till I've finished. It's a bit like I'm talking to a brick wall with holes for eyes. I feel I can't be bothered to see her anymore.

We are told that to be a good listener you should look at the person who is talking and avoid interrupting with your own ideas. It sounds as if Hannah does look at my friend and gives her the time to speak, but her blank stares and unresponsiveness communicate a message of disinterest and boredom.

Remembering the words we hear

One part of listening is not 'how' you do it (which we shall look into later in this chapter) but how much you remember of what someone has told you. When we report a conversation we have had, we often do so believing that we remember most of what has been said. This is far from the case because several studies have suggested that we only remember about 25–50% of what we hear. This means that if you talk or listen to parents for about ten minutes you and they will only really process and remember two and a half to five minutes worth of the information. Will they have heard and remembered the important bits? Similarly, how much will you have remembered of what the parents have said to you? How well do you listen?

You can try this out with a friend. Have a stopwatch ready and invite your friend to talk for five minutes, telling you about something like a recent holiday she has enjoyed. When the five minutes are up, repeat back to your friend, in as much detail as you can remember. It will be interesting to see how much detail you do manage to recall and how easy or difficult it was to do. However, it is then important to notice how each of you 'felt' during this activity. For you, the listener, it can be rather unsatisfactory (if you can't remember much detail) or it can leave you feeling smugly proud of your own memory skills. What is significant is that it will probably leave you feeling somewhat emotionally 'disconnected' from the speaker because you have been preoccupied with yourself and your own memory skills. When we *attend* only to *words* and *factual information* we actually *miss* most of the *message*. *True listening* involves far more than attending to the words spoken because it is about making an *emotional connection* with the other person.

A tip to help memory and concentration

Sometimes it is important that you do attend to the words and the facts that someone is telling you. If you find it particularly difficult to concentrate on what someone is saying, then try repeating the words mentally as they are spoken, as this will reinforce the message and help you control the mind drift.

What does listening involve?

- It is about listening with your **ears** to the actual words being said, rather than hearing what you 'think' is being said. It is all too easy to tune in to the first few words of the speaker and then make assumptions about what he might be talking about without even realising you are doing it. When you are listening with your ears you can also notice if the speech is hurried or slow, high pitched or deep, excitable or depressed. If you really listen for clues about how the person is feeling from the voice and speech of someone talking, you will be using your ears well.

- It is about listening with your **eyes** as you pay attention to the person who is talking. This means noticing the speaker's facial expressions: is the person looking happy, sad or angry? Your eyes can scan the person to look at her body language. Is she crossing her arms in a defensive posture, for example, or is she using lots of gestures? You can tell the mood of a person and what she might want to say just from looking at her. It is amazing how much you can convey or understand when communicating with someone using a foreign language simply by using your eyes.

- It is about listening with your **mind** for the real meaning behind the speaker's words. For example when someone says, 'It's okay', is that really so? Is that person actually trying to say, 'I don't want to do that' but does not want to offend you? To be a good listener is about listening for the 'unspoken' meanings behind the words. We are all engaging in this kind of indirectness in the way we communicate as a way of floating on top of an awkward situation. We need to be mentally alert to be a good listener, treating these messages as clues and where appropriate checking them out with the speaker.

- It is about listening with your **heart** to the other person, allowing compassion and empathy to flow through and showing respect. It is about paying attention to the other person's emotional state and responding to it appropriately. Parents sometimes come with considerable emotional 'content' and usually expect you, the practitioner, to be able to tune in immediately. If you are open-hearted, you will be quicker at picking up the true message behind the body language, the eye contact, the tone of voice, the words and all the other meta-messages that go on.

The seven personal qualities of the good listener

There are seven qualities to be aware of if you want to be a good listener, which will create a climate of trust and enable you to develop successful relationships.

1. Empathy, attunement and presence

This is the ability to get a sense of what someone else is feeling without the person actually saying so and to be able to respond with sensitivity. At the highest level, as

Goleman (1999) suggests, empathy is being able to understand the issues or concerns that lie behind another's feelings. It is about being able to put yourself in the other person's shoes and imagine what he must be feeling. You need to be able to 'forget yourself' as you tune in to how the other person is feeling. Attunement is when another person's emotions are met with empathy. Underlying empathy and attunement is the ability to sustain presence with another. Presence simply means being fully 'in the present' with another, using all your senses to notice the other person's mood and feelings through reading subtle messages coming from body posture, tone of voice, etc. Being able to pick up on emotional clues is particularly important in situations where people find it difficult to say what they are really feeling. This is examined in more detail in Chapter 9.

2. Warmth

Warmth is something that comes from the heart. It is not an intellectual skill that can be learnt through words. Warmth is having a genuine interest in other people, which is non-judgemental. It is our intellect that judges all the time. We need to make judgements sometimes in order to make decisions, but when you are truly listening to another person it is important to suspend that judgement and simply be open-hearted as well as open-minded.

3. Respect for others

Having respect for others means a belief in the inherent positive qualities of the person you are talking to. When you are listening and talking to a parent, you may not actually like him very much. However, you need to respect that the other person has feelings and belief systems just as you do and has a right to those views, however different they might be from your own.

4. Genuineness

Genuineness is another quality that comes from the heart but can be directed from the head, for it means having a true intention to be helpful and positive towards the parents you are engaging with. If you genuinely want to make a relationship with the other person, then that will come across and even if things go a 'bit wrong', they can quickly be resolved.

5. Sense of humour

This is very important in any relationship. In the professional context, if you have a sense of humour then that can ease tension if used appropriately and help parents gain a perspective on the things they might be worrying about. It can help reassure parents that you will be a source of delight to their children and that they can relax with you. Being able to laugh at yourself is viewed as an endearing quality in UK culture, as we know from the wealth of stand up comedians that perennially appear on our stages and television screens.

6. Sense of humility

However 'important' we might consider ourselves or others, at the end of the day we are all human, with human limitations. If we recognise this within ourselves, we shall have compassion for ourselves. This in turn is the gateway to having compassion for others. The trouble is that our ego often gets in the way. We often need to 'pretend' a sense of importance to ourselves as a way of feeling confident. However, the ego plays tricks on us, because self-importance blinds us to what is real. A genuine sense of humility is not about seeing ourselves as unimportant, but about recognising that whilst we are lovely, we can also make mistakes. We all make mistakes and that is part of how we learn as human beings.

7. Self-awareness

Self-awareness is about recognising and getting to know your own limitations and also knowing your own strengths. It is about becoming aware of what kind of person you are and the impact you have on other people when you meet and get to know them. If you are pursuing a career in the care and education of young children, it is vital that you are willing to explore your own 'inner' life as well as understanding what makes others tick.

Wearing the 'worried look'

When I was younger I was often told I was 'wearing the worried look'. It was an off-putting expression on my face and I was not even aware I was doing it. People made judgements about this expression. Some thought I was feeling annoyed or disapproving. Others thought I was afraid of them or anxious about the situation. People I did not know so well judged me as being awkward and distant. What was interesting was that they treated me 'as if' I was feeling these things even if I was not. It became a barrier to 'being myself' when in relationships with others.

When I looked at myself in the mirror, I could not make the expression, so I did not know what I looked like. It was only when I was caught on camera that I could see the face I was pulling. It dawned on me, when friends and family pointed out when I was doing it, that this 'worried look' came over my face when I was preoccupied with my own thoughts instead of paying full attention to the speaker. This look distanced me from others as my thoughts momentarily drifted away from the thread of the conversation. I was lost in my own reverie, which may have included anxiety, irritation or thoughts about what I might say or do next.

This 'worried look' became my mask of self-consciousness. It was the expression I inadvertently pulled when I was not fully at ease in a situation. Those situations often arose when I was part of an awkward family get-together, or when I had a meeting with my boss, or when I had to talk to an angry parent. When I felt my heart beating fast, or my palms became sweaty, or little scenarios played out in my head, the 'worried look' appeared. I wonder what your expression of self-consciousness looks like? You will have to ask someone you trust because you will not be aware of what you are doing.

The power of positive pretence

Once you know what you are doing, as I discovered, you can consciously work to overcome these off-putting mannerisms. I have visited many day nurseries, pre-schools and nursery schools and watched the off-putting looks and mannerisms that the practitioners give to the parents. They may avoid eye contact, look miserable, be overly cheerful in screechy high-pitched voices, have a surly manner, frown or look worried. These are just some of the 'self-conscious masks' I have seen. You may see others in your colleagues or your parents. People do not mean to come across as unfriendly or over-friendly. It is because of their lack of confidence and lack of self-awareness and the fact that they are thinking more about themselves than about the effect they are having on the people around them.

So how do we overcome these negative habits and self-conscious masks?

- **Think** about how you want to come across to others. Do you want to look professional and friendly at the same time? Be aware of what you want to look like. Self-awareness is the basis of all good communication and listening skills.
- **Smile** at the person you are listening to. There is a lot of truth in the expression 'the winning smile'. It is not only a look of triumph when we achieve something; it is also the look that wins good relationships. If you smile at someone you are communicating a welcome and an offer of goodwill. However, the smile needs to be genuine, allowing compassion to flow from you to the other person. A genuine smile is when you want to give the other person a good feeling.
- **Act** *as if* you are feeling confident, interested in the other person or want to be with the other person even if you do not. This is the *power of positive pretence*. If you are not feeling confident, for example, it is okay not to feel confident. However, you need to develop the skills of *looking* confident to overcome shyness and timidity. When you act 'as if' you are feeling confident, you will be amazed at how you actually begin to feel more confident. This is the basis of many of the current therapies such as solution focused therapy and cognitive behaviour therapy.

Barriers to listening

There will be times when you will not be listening well and there will be times when the parents you are talking to will not be listening to you very well either. Let us now consider those typical times that we all experience.

- When you are desperate to get your message across.
- When you are in a hurry.
- When you are anxious about what you have to say.
- When two people are talking at the same time.
- When the other person is being negative towards you.
- When you feel you are being interrupted, so your mind becomes preoccupied with your own thoughts.

The common theme of all these times is that you are not being able to express your feelings. As Stone, Patton and Heen (2000, p. 89) say: 'When people are having a hard time listening, often it is not because they don't know how to listen. It is, paradoxically, because they don't know how to express themselves well. Unexpressed feelings can block the ability to listen.' The reason is that it is very important to be open, honest and interested in the other person to be able to listen well. When you feel hurried, let's say, yet are unable actually to tell the other person you are in a hurry, your focus is thrown back on yourself. Instead of fully listening to the other person you are looking at the clock or working out how you can end the conversation. In the busy and rushed lives of today, many encounters between people are unsatisfactory, not because we are in a hurry but because we cannot tell the other person we are in a hurry!

Becoming an active listener

In the 1950s Carl Rogers developed his own therapeutic approach to counselling, which involved what he called 'active listening'. There are five key elements of active listening, which, if put into practice, ensure that you really hear and understand what the other person is saying and the other person knows you are hearing and understanding what she is saying.

You can develop active listening skills by following the steps outlined below. Whilst you might feel a little self-conscious at first, as you develop these skills they will become part of the way you relate to all people and you will find that your social skills will be vastly improved. You will also find that you will be more successful in your relationships with parents and they will be mutually much more satisfying. It takes a lot of concentration and determination to become an active listener because most of us have bad habits when it comes to listening and we all know how difficult it is to break bad habits.

1. Pay attention

First of all you need to give the speaker your undivided attention and acknowledge the message you are receiving. It is important to be attentive to the 'whole' person, as body language and tone of voice give you 93% of the message (Mehrabian 1971). What is not said speaks more loudly than the actual words!

How to do it

- Look at the speaker directly but avoid long stares as this can feel threatening.
- Put aside distracting thoughts such as mentally preparing your reply to what is being said.
- Avoid being distracted by environmental factors. In a busy nursery setting there will be plenty of distractions, so if you want to listen to a parent properly, take her to a quiet corner or even to another quiet room. If you are planning a meeting make sure that you will not be interrupted by the phone ringing and that the chairs are comfortable, for example.
- 'Listen' to the speaker's body language.
- Refrain from joining in or listening to side conversations, when listening in a group setting.

2. Show that you are listening

Recognising that most of a message comes through body language and gestures, you can actively show you are listening through what you consciously do and what facial expressions you give.

How to do it

- Nod occasionally.
- Smile and use other facial expressions that convey genuine interest.
- Note your posture and make sure it is open and inviting. If you stand with your arms crossed, for example, it communicates defensiveness and 'keep away' so let your arms hang more loosely.
- Encourage the speaker to continue with small verbal comments like 'yes' and 'uh huh'. Total silence on your part will silence the speaker.

3. Provide feedback

However well you think you are listening, you will distort what you hear according to your own assumptions, judgements and beliefs. In order really to understand the speaker's message your role is to reflect on what is being said, by maybe asking for clarification and asking questions.

How to do it

- Reflect on what has been said by paraphrasing. This means that you would start by saying something like 'What I'm hearing is . . .' or 'It sounds like you are saying . . .' and then paraphrase in your own words what you think the person has just said. You will then discover whether or not you have got the 'right end of the stick', as it were, together with giving the speaker a feeling of being truly valued and listened to.

- Ask questions to clarify certain points, such as 'What do you mean when you say . . .?' or 'Is this what you mean?'
- Summarise the speaker's comments from time to time. It will not only show you are listening but help you keep focused too. This is examined in more detail in Chapter 6.

4. Defer judgement

It has been mentioned before that it is easy to make judgements about what the speaker is saying. When that happens, interruption follows and it frustrates the speaker and the full understanding of the message will be lost.

How to do it

- Allow the speaker to finish. Sometimes it is worth leaving a little pause to see if the speaker wants to add anything more.
- Avoid interrupting with counter-arguments, solutions or inappropriate reassurance.
- Acknowledge your own emotional response to what someone is saying by saying so and asking for more information. For example, if you feel hurt or angry, you might want to say something like 'It may be that I have not quite understood you correctly and I find I am taking what you just said personally. What I thought you just said was . . .; is that what you meant?'

5. Respond appropriately

I have already mentioned that, to be a good listener, you need to be aware of seven personal qualities and it is these that will help you respond appropriately. You need to remember that active listening is a model for respect and understanding, which is at the heart of professionalism.

How to do it

- Be candid, open and honest in whatever type of response you give.
- Assert your opinions respectfully.
- Use the 'Golden Rule' of all major religions; that is to treat the other person as you, he or she would like to be treated.

Something to reflect upon

Here is an extract from a book of 'meditations' written by a spiritual teacher, who is currently inspiring millions of people all around the world. I have read this at many of my talks and workshops and the overwhelming positive response that I have always received means that I would like to share it with you now.

Listening

True listening is another way of bringing stillness into the relationship. When you truly listen to someone, the dimension of stillness arises and becomes an essential part of the relationship. But true listening is a rare skill. Usually, the greater part of the person's attention is taken up by their thinking. At best, they may be evaluating your words or preparing the next thing to say. Or they may not be listening at all, lost in their own thoughts.

True listening goes far beyond auditory perception. It is the arising of alert attention, a space of presence in which the words are being received. The words now become secondary. They may be meaningful or they may not make sense. Far more important than 'what' you are listening to is the act of listening itself, the space of conscious presence that arises as you listen. That space is the unifying field of awareness in which you meet the other person without the separative barriers created by conceptual thinking. And now the other person is no longer 'other'. In that space, you are joined together as one awareness, one consciousness.

From *Stillness Speaks* by Eckhart Tolle (2003, pp. 94–5)

CHAPTER 4

Developing personal and social competence

Emotional competence implies we have a choice as to how we express our feelings.

(Goleman 1999, p. 81)

It is an interesting notion that we can actually develop personal and social competence. How do we know if we are socially competent? How do we know how much we are aware of our little foibles and personal characteristics? I have always liked the wisdom of Socrates when he realised that the only thing he definitely did know was that he knew very little about anything! That wisdom makes me smile as I feel it is true for all of us. However, it is worth striving to be better at things, and if you are someone who is working with other people (and as teachers and practitioners, you most certainly are) the most important learning you can do is to be better at understanding yourself and getting along with others.

The basis of personal and social competence is about being aware of feelings and it underpins the very moral fabric of our society. As Sue Gerhardt states in her recent book *The Selfish Society* (2010, p. 310):

> The moral and emotional issues that we have to deal with as a society are the same as those we begin to grasp in the cradle: how we learn to pay attention to others and their feelings, how we manage conflict between people, and how we balance our own needs with the needs of others. Morality is about the way that we manage the interface between self and society, an interface that starts in babyhood and is learned from the actual practice of early relating. This gives early child-rearing a prime place in our cultural life.

You cannot underestimate the importance of your work in making relationships with babies and young children. And your competence in the way you relate to parents will strengthen that work immeasurably. In order to develop personal and emotional competence we need to be aware of, regulate and express our own feelings and we need to tune in to and acknowledge the feelings of others. This is the running thread throughout this book both at a theoretical and a skills level (in Part I) and in a more personal way through case study stories (in Part II). In this chapter we shall consider personal and social learning, together with what is meant by symbolic and non-symbolic communication.

Being aware of your ego

As we begin to pay attention to how we feel about things, how our whole body responds when we become emotionally aroused, that is the beginning of developing self-awareness. If someone begins to get angry with you, how does it make you feel? Does it make you angry back or does it make you fearful or distressed? Does it make you more determined to stand your ground or do you feel like running away? Your emotional responses are telling you something about yourself. However, a much more important question you might want to ask yourself is this: 'Is this really me, or is this how I have learned to behave?'

The voice of the ego

Developing personal competence is about paying attention to the voice of the ego. The ego is a term that is often tossed about in general conversation but we do not usually think about what the term really means. It is commonly referred to when we criticise someone as being arrogant or big headed and describe him as having 'an over-inflated ego'. Indeed the term ego has various meanings. It was originally used by Freud, who was the founder of psychoanalysis, to describe the self-conscious and rational aspect of oneself. It was then Carl Jung who took these ideas and developed them further. However, in the context of this book I would describe the ego as the little voice in our heads that casts judgements.

We are all born without an ego; we are simply virgin consciousness. A little baby has no sense of self; initially he does not distinguish himself as separate from his mother. However, as the months pass the baby arrives at a sense of self, which is the start of his developing ego. I remember watching with great delight when my son, at about seven or eight months old, became very excited and animated when he realised that the reflection in the mirror was himself.

As we develop as children, our ego is created by what others think of us. We might be told 'What a beautiful child you are', or maybe 'You are very stupid', or 'You are a mean person', or 'You have real talent.' Other people's opinions shape the way we see ourselves. That is the ego at work. The essence of the opinions of others is the ego. Our sense of who we are becomes a reflection of what others think. If a baby receives a positive nurturing experience in the Early Years, then this becomes the template about how he views himself as well as others. He sees himself in a positive light and he also sees the world around him as a benign place. He has a strong and positive ego. However, if a baby experiences neglect or is cared for in an inconsistent or even hostile way he develops a less positive view about himself and the world and his ego is more negative. We have all had both positive and negative experiences in our lives that influence our judgements. The trouble is that the judgemental 'voice' of the negative ego aspect can disconnect us from our own simple beauty, strength and originality.

I was brought up being told by my mother that she 'knew best' and that I did not know anything. Whilst her 'knowledge' might have been reassuring when I was very little and needed her guidance and care, as I got older my mother resorted to this stance as her way of controlling me. This message interfered with my self-confidence and ability to have my own ideas without feeling guilty. The trouble was the little voice in my head kept telling me that I did not know anything and I began to believe it. This was the negative aspect of my ego taking a hold. It has taken a great deal of effort on my part to work on my own personal competence to overcome the crippling anxiety of self-doubt that even to this day creeps in when I am feeling stressed.

The Emotional Competence Framework

In the introduction we referred to Daniel Goleman's work where he made the important links between intelligence, learning and emotion and called it Emotional Intelligence (1996). In a later book, Goleman (1999) created what he calls the 'Emotional Competence Framework'. We feel that this encapsulates the overall differences between personal and social competence. However, it is important to recognise that we do not treat them separately as they both need to work together. Personal and social competence are simply different aspects of our emotional intelligence. Here is Goleman's framework summarised below;

Personal competence

- Self-awareness – knowing one's internal states, preferences, resources and intuitions.
- Self-regulation – managing one's internal states, impulses and resources such as trustworthiness, conscientiousness and adaptability.
- Motivation – emotional tendencies that guide or facilitate reaching goals, such as commitment, initiative and optimism.

Social competence

- Empathy – awareness of others' feelings, needs and concerns, which has been discussed in detail in Chapter 8.
- Social skills – adeptness at inducing desirable responses in others, such as co-operation, conflict management and leadership.

Personal and social competence is a key element in being able to make sense of and take control of our lives, whether professionally or personally. It is something we can always develop further, and if we are prepared see it as a skill and to practise it, then it will enhance our confidence and pleasure in everything we do.

Interpersonal skills stem from self-awareness, knowledge and understanding and are not confined to any single aspect of our lives. We communicate interpersonally every time we interact with others. How effective we are reflects how skilful we are. How skilful do you think you are?

Four stages of competence

Reflecting back on the wisdom of Socrates, it is worth thinking about how we learn anything. I rather like the framework called the 'four stages of competence' which Bert Decker (1989) attributes to Abraham Maslow (although this model does not appear in Maslow's major works). You might like to think about these stages in relation to your own life and skills.

Stage one: unconscious incompetence – we don't know that we don't know

Imagine a small child in your setting wants to 'do writing' like you do. He does not realise that he does not yet know how to write. He gets a pencil and starts to make marks on the paper declaring that this is his 'writing'. I wonder how much you have thought about your effectiveness in getting on with other people. Most of us have probably not had much feedback about our interpersonal skills. We do not know how good or bad we are. We are not even aware of our interpersonal communication habits. We are in this state of unconscious incompetence.

Stage two: conscious incompetence – we know that we don't know

This same small child brings you his 'writing' for you to read. You say something to appease the child but he realises that you can't read his writing; that his writing isn't proper writing after all. He has moved to stage two where he knows that he doesn't know. When have you discovered you are not competent at something? It can sometimes come as a nasty shock. How well, for example, do you greet parents at the beginning of the day, especially the 'difficult' parents?

Stage three: conscious competence – we work at what we don't know

This is when we consciously decide to make the effort to learn a new skill. Maybe this is why you have decided to read this book? Learning and improving any skill involves effort and practice. The small child begins to learn how to write the letters of his name. He learns how to hold his pencil and practises this writing over and over again, seeking feedback from you. Maybe you want to practise your skills so you can feel completely at ease when you greet parents as they arrive with their children in the morning.

Stage four: unconscious competence – we don't have to think about knowing it

This is when the skill is so well established that you do it without consciously thinking about it. It has become 'second nature'. The small child can now write his name without help or laborious effort. You smile and greet each parent in a way that just suits each one, feeling completely comfortable and without having to concentrate on whether or not you are smiling or saying 'the right thing'.

Symbolic and non-symbolic communication

In their recent book on communication with parents, Taylor Dyches, Carter and Prater (2012) distinguish the difference between symbolic and non-symbolic communication. The more awareness we have about the numerous ways we convey a message to someone, the more we can consciously use that awareness to develop our interpersonal skills. Let us consider, then, what is meant by symbolic and non-symbolic communication.

Symbolic communication

This is where we communicate with one another using some form of 'symbol' to represent language or mental ideas. Examples of these would include written language, picture-based systems and sign language. When we are talking to one another it is the speech we use that becomes the symbolic communication. The four main verbal symbolic communication skills are;

- **Word choices**. How formal or technical is your language with parents? It can be very off-putting if jargon is used that they do not understand. When you are trying to say something important it can be difficult to strike the right balance between giving gentle hints to someone, and therefore coming across as unclear, and being direct, which can seem rude to someone who is not used to it.
- **Assertiveness**. This is using language in a clear, unambiguous and confident manner. Assertiveness can often be confused with being aggressive.
- **Negotiation**. This is the skill of being assertive and guiding parents towards a mutually agreeable decision, by setting boundaries on things like talking time and subject matter and focusing on solutions rather than problems.
- **Active listening**. This is an area of communication that is discussed in detail in Chapter 3 and is vital for good interpersonal skills.

Non-symbolic communication

This covers the more subtle aspects of communication such as body language and is much more open to misinterpretation as styles vary from culture to culture and even between families. Non-symbolic forms of communication are also often unconsciously expressed, which means we may not even be aware of the messages we give or how they are being received. A 'posh' accent may give others the impression that the speaker is wealthy and 'stuck up' when in actual fact that person could be financially poor and very easy going. The three main non-symbolic communication skills are;

- **Paralanguage**. This refers to the messages we receive from signals given by the voice, such as accent, articulation, pitch and volume. For example a low voice communicates greater dominance, yawning might convey boredom and sighs can communicate impatience. Our impression of rudeness and politeness are often based on subtle variations in pitch. For example a small shift in vocal pitch can make us feel someone is questioning our abilities. However, shifts in pitch also indicate 'turn taking' cues in a conversation too.

- **Timing**. This refers to things like pacing, pauses, silences, turn taking and how much time we give to an exchange. These aspects contribute to a conversation feeling either hurried or relaxed. As you become more skilled at using pacing skills, you will be able to manage your professional relationships (such as time bonded meetings with parents) without feeling pressurised. In this way you will give the parents the feeling they are the most important people in the world.

- **Body language**. This includes *body movement* such as wagging a finger and rolling one's eyes indicating annoyance or exasperation. *Touch* such as rubbing your forehead or crossing your arms can indicate thoughtfulness or defensiveness. Touch also includes touching other people like shaking hands; depending on the circumstances, this can indicate either a warm welcome or more distant formality. *Personal space* is another interesting form of body language. How near should we be when talking to someone else? It can be very close within a family, but in the work setting around one metre distance is usually comfortable for an informal chat but it needs to be around two metres when sitting down for a more formal meeting. This is especially so if you are meeting that person for the first time. *Personal appearance* is a very important aspect of body language, which will be discussed in more detail below. *Body posture* and *eye contact* are other forms of body language that will also be examined later in the chapter.

Dress and personal appearance

When we meet someone for the very first time we form immediate and vivid impressions of her within the first five seconds. This is an instant emotional response that happens far quicker than our rational minds work. Although our view of the person develops as we get to know her, that first impression is incredibly important and is what we tend to remember.

These impressions are formed by what we can see, which are mainly the face, hair and clothing. Whether or not you wear make-up (as a female) or a beard (as a male) will influence what others think of you. It also communicates to others how you feel about yourself. It is of vital importance to be aware of your personal appearance in your professional life. You must not under-estimate the impact you have on both parents and children alike in the way you take care of your appearance.

Feel at ease

The most important thing is that you feel at ease with the way you look. There is no right or wrong way (unless there are particular rules about uniform, beards or make-up in your setting) to dress or groom. However, unless you feel comfortable, you will not come across to others as comfortable and so you will not communicate with others so well.

Taking care

Whilst it is important to feel at ease, there is a difference between taking care and not bothering with your appearance. Make sure that your hair is washed and brushed, and if you wear make-up enjoy putting it on. Even if you wear a uniform that is casual, take care that it is not crumpled when you put it on first thing in the morning and make sure that it looks clean at the start of the day. These small details will go a long way in helping you to feel good and to help gain the trust and respect of parents.

Wearing a uniform

It is customary these days that most practitioners wear a uniform in many of the Early Years settings. The uniform is usually a coloured sweatshirt or fleece with a logo and maybe your name embroidered on it. If you are in a position to choose the colour of your uniform, be mindful of the effect that colour can have on yourself, the children and the parents. Although black is the 'fashion' for a lot of people, I personally find that black sweatshirts look very drab, especially for the children, as they like colour. Also, light colours show the dirt easily; when you are dealing with paint, dough, food, runny noses, moving equipment about and much more besides, it is easy to look a bit grubby if you wear something like a white or light blue shirt.

If you do wear a uniform, wear it with pride because it will communicate how you feel about being a professional. It also helps you to look and feel part of a team. If you can choose what you wear be mindful of getting the right balance between being comfortable yet also smart.

A little story

Our attitudes towards dress and appearance develop, as everything else, in early childhood. I remember my daughter at age two or three went through a phase of only wearing pretty dresses followed by a phase of only wearing trousers! This reflected her wish first to be a 'princess' all the time followed by a period of wanting to play as a tomboy with her older brother. Our views about dress do change with experience. However, here is an amusing little story I was told at a conference a few years ago.

I was going to a posh dinner with my husband one evening and he had dressed in his dinner jacket. As we came downstairs to leave our son said to him, 'Daddy, don't wear that!' My husband asked him why not. 'Well every time you wear those clothes the next morning you have a headache and are not very well.' He associated the clothing with a hangover and thought that one caused the other!

Body posture and eye contact

Body posture

The way we move our bodies tells others a lot about how we are feeling in any given social situation. If you want to engage the attention and interest of someone else, it is more effective to be fluid rather than rigid in one's movements. Stiffness conveys rigid thinking and defensiveness, whilst awkward movements convey insecurity and submission.

Confidence is expressed through an upright body posture. We can be more assertive when we are standing rather than sitting. If you stand up you will feel more confident. By being aware of this it will also make you more sensitive to the feelings of those parents who are physically disabled and confined to a wheelchair, or who cannot stand for long and so sit down to talk with you. If you find yourself in such a situation then it is important that you sit down as well, so that you are at eye level with the other person and there is mutuality in the exchange.

Next time, when you are standing and talking with a parent, notice if you tend to stand on one hip and rock when you are talking. If you do, then you are inadvertently communicating that you are bored and feeling impatient. If you lean against a wall and cross your legs at the ankles then that comes across as sloppy rather than casual. Paying attention to these little details could change how you feel about yourself as well as improve the quality of your interactions in the workplace.

Eye contact

In the UK culture it is important to make eye contact with the person you are having a conversation with. Most of us know this. However, making eye contact is not the same as making good eye communication. It is often said that if you look into someone's eyes you are looking into his soul. If someone were to look at you with an intense stare that felt too long it could actually feel as if you have been assaulted.

Indeed Decker (1989) refers to the three I's of eye contact as being:

- Intimacy – looking at someone for a long period, that is, from ten seconds to one minute to convey love and affection.
- Intimidation – looking at someone for a long time, that is, from ten seconds to one minute to elicit fear.

- Involvement – over 90% of our communication with others (especially in the workplace) simply calls for involvement when we look at someone for five to ten seconds before looking away.

In my work with autistic children and teenagers, even making that five to ten second eye contact can be uncomfortable and even 'painful' to many of them. We may also find this is the case when we have a difficult meeting with a parent. An autistic teenager recently told a group I was working with that he had heard of a simple tip to cope with eye contact. He said that he looks at the centre of a person's forehead just above the eyebrows. Why not try this for yourself if you find yourself in a situation when eye contact feels difficult. You might also want to observe others and notice how an individual's eye contact patterns make you feel about her.

There are so many cues in communication, but it is hoped that this chapter will have aroused your interest to become more observant of yourself and others as the first step in improving your own interpersonal skills. It is an exciting process because other people really do respond positively if you make an effort to connect with them with genuine warmth and interest and without judgement.

CHAPTER 5

How to feel OK

Transactional Analysis (also known as TA) is a technique for studying interactions between individuals. It has been successfully employed by therapists, psychologists and managers for the past fifty years to help with self-development and to improve interpersonal skills. TA enables you to understand yourself better. Through awareness and observation of how you behave towards different people in different situations, it creates a feeling of freedom. It offers you the freedom of choice about 'how' you interact with someone else. The idea of TA was originally developed by Eric Berne in the early 1960s, before becoming popularised by one of his students, Thomas Harris, who wrote the book *I'm OK – You're OK* in 1967.

You do not need to know all the psychological theory to be able to apply some of the principles, but some knowledge and background will help you make better sense of how and why it works. It is always best to experiment with any new communication tool on someone you know well (and whom you trust) to see if it works. It is no good just reading about something, you need to try it out for yourself. Communication is after all an art and not a firm science. All the techniques and observations throughout this book offer you a broad framework. However, it is up to you to create the colours and make your own picture with your own unique personality and behavioural style.

What I find fascinating about the TA model is that it so elegantly fits with John Bowlby's attachment theory, as well as with current neurological research about how the brain works. I will weave a little of the Attachment model through the text so you can see the threads of connection.

Defining a transaction

Berne described the behaviours that happen between two people when they talk together as *transactions*. He said that a transaction was 'the fundamental unit of social intercourse'. If two people encounter one another, then one person will inevitably start to speak. Berne called this the 'transactional stimulus'. The other person will then respond in some way that relates to what the first person said, which Berne called the 'transactional response'.

Whilst that seems straightforward, the interesting part of Berne's ideas came out of his observations of patients in therapy, as well as people generally interacting with one another in groups. Harris and Bjork (1986, p. 12) describe a particular patient who influenced Berne's theories;

> In the 1950's TA's founder Dr. Eric Berne was treating a patient who was a lawyer. At one point the lawyer said, 'Right now I feel like a little boy'. And he looked like a little boy, the way he was sitting, his vocabulary, his facial expression. Soon the treatment began to center on the question, 'Who's talking now, the lawyer or the little boy?' They were two different people. About six months later Berne introduced his observation that still another person made his appearance in the present. That was a person who was very much like the man's father, a parental person who appeared in a nurturing, sometimes critical way.

In essence, transactional analysis is based on the observation that we are all functioning as three people in one: a child, a parent and an adult. Eric Berne described these three different aspects as ego states, but so as the term is not confused with other definitions of the ego, I will refer to them as 'modes'.

Parent mode, Child mode and Adult mode

The Parent mode can be described as the 'recordings in the brain' that were received by you in the first five years of your life, given to you, not just by your parents but by all significant adults. These 'recordings' will encompass what adults said to you and the observations you made of their behaviour before you had the rational awareness to discern this input. It is like the ego that was described in the previous chapter, as the Parent mode encompasses attitudes and judgements, both positive and negative.

The Parent mode can be recognised as the following:

- Being nurturing and sympathetic.
- Giving praise.
- Giving warnings and punishments.
- Being critical.
- Making accusations.

The Parent mode is *not* about actually being a parent; it is merely the descriptive term for this behavioural style that was given originally by Eric Berne.

The Child mode also reflects the experiences you had in the first five years of life, but this time it is responding to the 'emotional recordings'. As Harris and Bjork (1986, p. 16) puts it, 'The most potent internal events were feelings.'

The Child mode can be recognised as the following:

- Being curious.
- Being intuitive and spontaneous.

- Being creative and enthusiastic.
- Being selfish and filled with desire.
- Being fearful.

Similarly, the Child mode is *not* about actually being a child; it is merely the descriptive term for this behavioural style.

The Adult mode also starts in infancy and is when you began to learn directly from your own experiences, rather than simply observing (Parent mode) or feeling (Child mode). It was when you discovered for yourself that a hot oven burned or that you could put a pair of boots on by yourself. You won't necessarily remember these experiences in your conscious mind, but your brain has 'recorded' the experience as learning from 'doing it by yourself'.

The Adult mode can be recognised as the parts of us that:

- Can reason.
- Can think.
- Can predict.
- Can solve problems.
- Can be present in the here and now.

The Adult mode is *not* about being an adult because infants under the age of one begin to function in this mode; it is merely the descriptive term for this behavioural style.

Understanding the different modes in action

Every time we have a conversation with someone we are likely to be shifting from one mode to another. I remember when I was working as an educational psychologist for an education authority and much of my time was spent visiting local schools. I enjoyed the relationships I had made with most of the head teachers and felt relaxed with them. However, there was one head teacher whom I liked and admired (she was very organised and 'professional') but somehow I felt uneasy about our relationship.

I always felt summoned, rather than invited into her office, and whilst she would comment on how smart I looked, she also remarked how she did not like sloppily dressed professionals. At that time I wore a suit for formal occasions. I made sure I always wore a suit when I visited this particular school! During our discussions this woman would be at great pains to tell me how good her school was before she then launched into the problems she was facing and that she expected me to sort out. Each time I was with her I felt like a foolish child. It would take enormous effort not to feel rather frightened of her, so I 'pretended' I was more confident than I felt. I would acknowledge her school was well run and would express appreciation that she was so well organised. A strange thing then happened; this woman would begin to tell me about her elderly mother, who had come to live with her and was being very difficult. Suddenly, I found myself seeing this woman turn from 'scary schoolteacher' to vulnerable 'little girl' as she opened herself up to me and wanted my support. This pattern of exchange seemed to happen on a regular basis before we were both able to get to the business of my visit.

From a TA perspective this head teacher took on the 'critical' Parent mode whenever she first met me. She behaved in ways that were powerful, intimidating, controlling and prejudiced. I then responded in the 'fearful' Child mode. My heart was pounding and I felt foolish and did not know what to say except to agree with everything this lady said. However, when I made positive comments about her school I unwittingly went into 'nurturing' Parent mode and in an instant this head teacher responded in Child mode towards me.

However, if we had remained in these seesawing Parent–Child modes we would not have been able to get on very well with the business of examining the concerns of the head teacher about certain children in her school and the ways I might have been able to offer assessment or support. We needed to get into Adult–Adult modes to work successfully together as two professionals so that we could think and reason and collaborate in imaginative problem solving.

The problem of the Parent–Child modes of communication

When you are talking to someone in a professional capacity you will get on far better if you are able to develop and sustain Adult–Adult modes of relating. However, as much of the time we are responding to our feelings and the feelings of others, it is easy to find ourselves unwittingly caught in the Parent or Child mode.

Sometimes parents come to us for help and support; they are seeking our understanding and care. It is easy to slip into Parent mode without even realising it! In the story of the first-time young mother in Chapter 8 on empathy and attachment, the female midwife took on the role of critical Parent by telling her to 'pick herself up'. In response the young mother took on the fearful Child mode and could not think of any questions to ask for fear she would be thought of as stupid. However, as the male midwife simply sat and listened, he was able to establish her trust and the young mother was able to find her Adult mode and begin to think and talk about her concerns.

Many professionals in positions of authority take on the Parent mode and then infantilise their colleagues or clients. Similarly, in your work, the parents of the children you work with may sometimes take on the Parent mode and infantilise you. However, taking on the critical Parent mode is a sign that someone is not as confident as she might want to believe she is; it is a defensive position.

The fussy parent

Over the years I have met practitioners who have expressed both distress and frustration with certain parents whom they describe as 'fussy'. Maybe these parents are making demands about 'special arrangements' for their child, such as only using the child's own cup or not being allowed to get dirty. These parents are probably anxious about leaving the child in the setting but are unable either to recognise or to articulate this. Instead of being clear about their worries or concerns, they go into 'fussy' or critical Parent mode. It is then easy for the practitioner either to get into a submissive Child mode or to match the parent and get into critical Parent mode. Either way, the communication becomes fraught with underlying agitation as the 'special arrangements' are focused on instead of the very real parental concerns that the child will be alright, separated from them and from the familiar routines and objects at home.

The new parent

In the story of Memhet's mother, described in Chapter 7, it was the practitioner who went into Parent mode as she put pressure on the mother to leave her crying son saying, 'Because he's fine once you've gone.' The mother desperately tried to cope with her distress and reacted in all the three modes at different times over the next few occasions. In the end she described her relationship with the staff as 'strained' because sadly the staff of the nursery were unable to communicate in the Adult mode. They will have had good intentions. They wanted Memhet to settle just as his mother wanted him to, but the modes of communication between this mother and the staff got stuck in judgements, confusion and distress.

The four life positions

Another aspect of Harris's TA framework is the concept of the four life positions. It is a fascinating further dimension about how to understand the way we behave towards one another. It also echoes the four attachment styles as described by Ainsworth *et al.* (1978), who developed Bowlby's theory of Attachment. These attachment styles are also described in relation to the TA model by Howe *et al.* (1999).

However, it must be said that my descriptions to follow are a very brief summary of Harris's ideas and must be read with care. It is suggested that you read the original texts for a better understanding. It is easy to oversimplify something that 'rings true' and then apply it clumsily in all sorts of social situations. With the exception of those people who are the most extreme cases, we operate in all four of the life positions. However, most of us do tend to use a particular lens through which we see the world most of the time.

How relationships affect our life positions

The relationships we make, throughout our lives, can enhance and also undermine our sense of security and confidence. This is both optimistic and pessimistic. In the context of this book, it is optimistic in that the positive and trusting relationships we, as professionals, make with parents can help them to feel more OK. In this more 'secure place' the parents are more likely to model accepting and attuned relationships with their own babies or young children. This then creates a positive cycle.

However, there is also a pessimistic side to this which creates a negative cycle. If parents are 'difficult' with you and are having difficulties showing affection towards their own children, it is easy to slip into critical Parent mode or fearful Child mode with them. However, this just serves to reinforce the insecure attachments all round, with devastating consequences for the babies and children as they grow up.

Holding these thoughts in mind, here are the four life positions, where they came from and how they 'show' themselves in interactions with others. Alongside these are the four attachment styles that resemble these life positions.

The four life positions are:	*The four attachment styles are:*
1. I'm not OK – You're OK	Anxious/ambivalent attachment style
2. I'm not OK – You're not OK	Anxious/disorganised attachment style
3. I'm OK – You're not OK	Anxious/avoidant attachment style
4. I'm OK – You're OK	Secure attachment style

The first three positions are based on feelings and we are not consciously aware of them. The fourth position is a conscious position because it is based on thought, belief and conscious action.

I'm not OK – You're OK

Harris maintained that we are all born with a sense of well-being but very early on in life every child concludes, 'I'm not OK' but his caregivers 'are OK'. Every time an infant's cries are not responded to or when an adult says 'no' to a young child, it quickly registers at an unconscious level as 'I'm not OK.' This is the human experience because we cannot 'reason' when we are very young; this 'I'm not OK' position is a deep-seated feeling rather than a conscious opinion of oneself. It then gets reinforced by the conditional love of parents when they say things like, 'I will love you if you stop screaming . . . eat your dinner . . . do your homework.'

People in this position are eager, willing and compliant to the demands of others without consideration for themselves. They always do things to seek others' approval. They are often the unhappy achievers in life. This life position reflects the 'anxious/ambivalent' attachment style.

I'm not OK – You're not OK

This position develops in infancy if a child's needs are consistently unmet by her caregivers. If a small child is unable to rely on getting comfort when he needs it he will begin to get a sense that the caregivers are 'not OK' either. The trouble is that if this position becomes entrenched a young child will either refuse comfort from his caregivers or seek to withdraw to comfort herself. You may have seen children like this in your own settings. This is why it is so important to develop nurturing relationships with the children in your care and positive relationships with their parents.

Many of the people in this position are those who have been abused or neglected as children and commonly find any intimacy or a show of care difficult to handle. These are the people who often seek comfort through making money, taking drugs, having sex or eating food. They are also the type of people who tend to avoid putting themselves out for others. This life position reflects the 'anxious/disorganised' attachment style.

I'm OK – You're not OK

This is the most worrying position as it usually comes from repeated abuse in early childhood. A young child no longer seeks comfort through his relationship with others but refuses to give up, and in order to feel OK he becomes tough. However, he then begins to show his toughness as a way of managing in the world. When things go wrong it is always someone else's fault. I have seen children in some group settings who are like this: aggressive and unable to receive adult comfort when they are hurt. They are the ones who need a lot of sensitive handling and care because they will push you away and can present as 'unlovable'. Similarly their parents may also be like this because of their own early experiences. It is easier to know how to support and communicate with these kinds of parents if we understand them better.

People in this life position feel they are always in the right and find it difficult to take responsibility when something goes wrong. Such people are likely to find it 'difficult to trust in the collective process of democratic decision making' (Gerhardt 2010, p. 285). These people want to take the law into their own hands. The caricature figures of the 'godfather' in many films portray this life position. This life position reflects the 'anxious/avoidant' attachment style.

I'm OK – You're OK

This is the position of hope. It is the position where we start in life because when a baby is born all is OK. If a baby's needs are met with the care of sensitive and attuned caregivers, then this position can be maintained. As babies grow into children they will have this position reinforced if they have experiences whereby they can prove to themselves and to others their own worth. This comes from being recognised and appreciated by others as someone of value. If someone sees you as lovely, you feel lovely, and in loveliness you also become loving. It is so much easier to have the capacity for compassion and empathy when you have had the experience of unconditional love.

This is a conscious position and everyone can get to this position with conscious effort. It comes with the experience of communicating with others in the Adult mode *and* receiving responses in the Adult mode from others. The Adult mode enables you to recognise the Child and Parent modes in others and to choose not to respond in kind. However, in essence, the ability to communicate in the Adult mode comes from being loved, appreciated and accepted unconditionally.

People in this life position feel confident and secure and are able to develop and sustain supportive relationships. They can repair relationships when they break down and are able to pick themselves up when things go wrong in their lives. People in this life position are more self-aware and are more prepared to learn from their mistakes.

Getting to I'm OK and You're OK: how to create Adult–Adult modes of communication

In Chapter 6 there is a good description of how to structure a conversation between a key person and a parent. This structure illustrates in detail what it means to communicate in the Adult mode.

However, what do you do if you meet a parent who has got stuck in the Parent mode? The first question you need to ask yourself is, 'What am I doing that might make that person behave like that? Am I behaving in the Child or Parent mode myself?' These modes are very seductive and we can unwittingly react to other people's behaviour and attitudes (or vice versa) in an instant.

Let us imagine a situation that could arise. A parent is late picking up her child and she is in a hurry, but the child is not ready when she arrives. The parent complains about this. Below is a possible series of exchanges that could change the situation into an I'm OK – You're OK position and create the much wanted Adult–Adult exchange.

Parent: *Complains*: '*Sarah isn't ready and you can see I'm late.*'

Practitioner: *Acknowledges feelings*: '*I can see you're angry. I'll help you get Sarah ready now.*'

Parent: *Complains again*: '*You know how I don't like to rush Sarah and I'm in a hurry.*'

Practitioner: *Agrees and takes the parent seriously:* '*You're right! I know I should have been more prepared.*'

Draws the parent out: '*I wish all parents were as considerate about their children as you.*'

A further problem arises because Sarah's coat cannot be found.

> **Parent:** *Still agitated:* *'I've got my mother-in-law about to descend on me and this is the last thing I need.'*

> **Practitioner:** *Gets help:* *'I will get someone to help me find Sarah's coat.'*

> *Expresses understanding:* *'I can understand why you are in such a hurry.'*

> *Shows curiosity:* *'Does your mother-in- law live far away?'*

The coat is found and Sarah's mother begins to help her put it on and the two of them talk a little to Sarah. The mother begins to calm down and relax. Sarah is able to relax too.

> **Parent:** *Happy to chat:* *'Yes she has to come by train and I have to pick her up from the station. But she's a stickler for time and she likes everything to be perfect. It makes me rather tense.'*

> *Apologises:* *'I'm sorry I was a bit abrupt with you. I didn't mean it.'*

> **Practitioner:** *Acknowledges:* *'That's okay. I should have had Sarah ready for you anyway. At least you are both ready now and Sarah has had a lovely day. I will tell you about it when you come in next time and we are not in a rush.'*

This verbal exchange has probably lasted less than a couple of minutes or so. It could have turned into a moment of tension between the practitioner and the parent, which would have spoilt the end of a good day for Sarah. What actually happened was that the practitioner was able to acknowledge the mother's feelings, agree with her own error and sort it out with everyone feeling OK.

In Part II of this book you will be able to read the stories of several parents and practitioners and have the chance to make more sense, in a living context, of the TA framework, as well as all the other theoretical models that have been described in Part I.

Communication skills in context

How to give shape and meaning to conversations with parents and carers in Early Years settings

Sometimes it feels like the staff at the nursery are so busy with all the children that there is no time for a proper conversation about the things that are on my mind about Sam. Often, important conversations turn into 'quick chats' when I am either arriving or leaving with him. I wish there was more time. If there was more time, I think I would feel more confident about talking to staff who are looking after him and feel more a part of things.

Structure is an everyday skill which is transferable

Most of us are on a daily basis familiar with the wish to establish a good partnership with parents and carers. It is an authentic way of sharing in the development of each child and his emotional and social growth and learning. We have discussed how important it is to build trust and rapport with parents in order for practitioners to become a 'secure base' (Bowlby 1988) for each child. The parent being included in this 'triangle of trust' (Goldschmied and Selleck 1996) is built by good daily contact and practice within the context of a welcoming atmosphere.

In this chapter we will consider the question of how to conduct a conversation with a parent or carer away from the demands of a busy setting. We need structure in many aspects of our life in order to have something to grasp hold of when we are doing things. By adding structure to our parental meetings we can feel more confident about our conversations. It also helps us to become more reflective about the process we are involved in and is good use of our precious time.

Structure is an everyday skill which is transferrable. We might think about a daily activity like going on a weekly food shop. What do you do first?

- Check your cupboards and the fridge to see what needs replacing.
- Write a shopping list.
- Go with your shopping list to the supermarket.

We often find that by doing this we are more focused and more likely to buy what we need rather than making impulsive purchases.

These models of intelligent thinking, which help us prepare ahead of a task, are not new approaches when working with people. Offering a structure helps us to share effectively a time-limited exchange. In an Early Years setting it is about exploring mutual expectations, in the interests of the child. It helps to establish respect, trust and goodwill between both parties. We will look in more detail later in this chapter at how the key principles of a good framework for conversations with parents may help guide practitioners in their initial and subsequent conversations with parents.

The reflective practitioner

It might be worth pausing for a moment and thinking about the kinds of conversations you are currently having in your setting. What might be the changes you hope to make to the way you currently conduct conversations about children with parents? Why does your team wish to make these changes? With a framework, clear boundaries and shared expectations in place, do you think both parties might feel happier about having 'open conversations'?

As a practitioner, would it help to create a space to think at each stage of the meeting? These questions are intended to encourage you to pause and really think about whether the conversations you are currently having are really improving outcomes for children. Having a clear approach can offer a map at times when a meeting may appear to have gone off track. It might also mean that parents can give their full attention to the 'here and now'. Conversations on the move can make us protective of ourselves and defensive because there are no boundaries.

Starting to have an open dialogue with parents may bring with it both a good deal of expectation and also a degree of anxiety. As a practitioner wishing to work in a new way there is a necessary commitment to be made. One has to make an active shift in one's mind from being a busy practitioner doing all that is required in that role. This may include becoming more aware of when it is appropriate to have brief exchanges at the beginning and ending of sessions and when something more is required: creating a more structured space where listening to a parent requires greater awareness and attunement. Key to this process is giving time to making it work. Approaches which invite this kind of partnership are based on shared ownership of decision making. Everybody's aspirations are respected, acknowledged and used as a basis for dialogue.

Some of the outcomes may include a greater shared understanding of problems, priorities and new possibilities. Agreed achievable and sustainable progress can be more successfully monitored. Achievements, strengths and shared learning can be celebrated together. How wonderful, too, to consider that Early Years staff by being skilled in this way of working with parents might be offering a first good experience of professional collaboration. This might impact on parents for the rest of their child's education.

The wider education system has from time to time been encouraged to be more inclusive when it comes to including parents in discussions about the outcomes they aspire to for their children. This has been especially true in the area of special education needs. However, in the field of Early Years practice there are excellent examples, as in the Sure Start initiatives, of actively seeking ways to engage with parents. These initiatives have challenged trans-generational expectations about what each child might achieve. Early Years practice in this area can offer a positive experience for parents, which raises and encourages expectations and which they can carry with them into the wider education system

What practitioners say at workshops about their ability to work closely with parents

- It's not a part of my job I feel skilled enough to do.
- It is for my manager or the SENCO to have such meetings.
- We do not have any training in this area.
- I don't have time.
- I wouldn't have enough confidence to know where to begin.
- I am worried about making parents feel like I might be criticising them in some way.
- Some parents can feel intimidating so I prefer to keep them at arm's length.

By offering a framework to our parent meetings we can address some of these concerns and anxieties. It is worth considering when it might be suitable to offer such a session to a parent. It might be good to have an individual time-bonded conversation before a child is fully on roll and important information requires to be gathered. It might help alleviate any early anxieties for the parent to do with separation in the early days. Mutual respect and trust is likely to be established through such a meeting and a plan for the first sessions can be shared. Time given to parents in this way may mean that staff have a better chance of really developing their knowledge of their key child.

Another time that it might be appropriate to have such a conversation is when there is a need to share sensitively some important documented observations of their child. Staff wishing to develop greater collaboration between home and the setting can actively monitor any improvements in this area by asking for feedback. Additionally, a practitioner may wish to raise a concern about a learning difficulty, special educational need or behavioural concern. Staff by meeting regularly in this way can build upon their professional relationship through regular discussion about monitoring progress and next steps in learning and development.

More sensitive issues such as when parental views relating to discrimination and diversity become voiced by the child in the setting may require additional thought and time. A meeting with a specific framework can provide a good opportunity to re-affirm the nursery's values and ethos, and ensure they are being jointly shared and celebrated. It might be worth adopting a similar approach at parent evenings and seeing whether staff would welcome having greater guidance on the structure to such meetings. It goes without saying that offering such an approach requires commitment, and skilful and energetic staff. However, planning for sincere and meaningful conversations with parents may prove to be mutually satisfying.

Figure 6.1 *The nursery practitioner sensitively reassures a mother, whose little girl is anxious about being left in the nursery.*

What might parents gain from such a conversation?

Parents want to be able to share their unique knowledge of their child. They wish, on the whole, to contribute to future aspirations of their children. Being listened to away from the busyness of the nursery allows them to share their thoughts and ideas about how best to support their child consistently and effectively. It sends an important message about working things out together.

What might practitioners hope to gain from such a conversation?

Sharing a good dialogue supported by a structure offers an opportunity to practise the core skills required to listen effectively (see Chapter 3). These skills can be practised with other staff, and training opportunities can be developed to improve better communication with hard to reach parents. By working in this way staff can learn at a deeper level about their key children's needs. A wider and deeper knowledge of both families and children will help build confidence on both sides.

What are the key principles for engaging successfully with parents so that children make progress?

How often have you sat in a meeting and asked yourself what is the point of the meeting? Recognising how careful wording will help you communicate the purpose of a meeting will lessen this kind of discomfort. The dominant aspects of communication are tone of voice, facial expression and body language. Listening to parents and giving time to the process is key to success in this way of working. Once you have practised the approach several times you will begin to see how setting clear parameters for the dialogue and an agreed purpose is just about being prepared in intelligent ways.

Planning ahead to engage parents in a discussion about their child

Context is all important and so it is essential to identify a place where parents are going to feel comfortable to share openly. Giving thought to the surroundings, the furniture and the decor, and considering whether to have some positive visual images up, which reflect the ethos of the setting, can be helpful. Sitting somewhere, uninterrupted by the demands and noise of the setting, can be a challenge, but a simple 'Do not disturb' sign for the door of the room will help!

The importance of focusing oneself prior to the conversation

Building in some time alone before the parent or carer arrives allows you to gather your thoughts, noticing your own body language and whether you feel any discomfort. Giving yourself this bit of time during a busy day allows you to welcome someone in a calm, composed manner. However, if you feel slightly anxious, preparing yourself by breathing slowly allows you to develop your concentration and wisdom. Following a structure helps also to alleviate any anxiety which may accompany such a task, especially if it is the first time you have conducted such a conversation

Getting started

It is not the aim of such a conversation with a parent to be therapeutic or concerned with the adult's emotional needs. It is specifically about developing the child's social and emotional development and learning. However, it is helpful to incorporate some of the simple tried and tested techniques from consultative approaches, time-limited counselling, solution focused therapy and coaching. It makes these private conversations with parents more client-centred.

We have talked about creating a comfortable and private space to conduct the meeting, so let us now turn to the face to face encounter. It is worth agreeing a verbal contract together at the start of the session. It is helpful at the commencement of a consultation to seek some clarification about the purpose of the conversation and, very importantly, what the parent or carer hopes to gain from the meeting. For example: 'I would like to find out as much as I can about Sam and about how you think we can help him with his sharing during free play. We have about 30 minutes, is that ok? I wonder what you are hoping for from our meeting today?' When you begin to explore together the purpose of the meeting, it is important to listen, observe and paraphrase, which is when, as you listen attentively and occasionally using your own words, you echo what has been said, expanding on the parent's ideas and feelings. It is important that the manner of the practitioner should be authentically curious and interested at this stage, e.g. 'It seems as though you are telling me that because Sam is an only child, he might find sharing difficult and that it is a skill we could together help strengthen in him.' Paraphrasing is powerful because it checks out that you have understood something correctly, and it communicates empathy and the fact that you have been listening. Reflecting back in this way needs to be as accurate as possible so you catch the right mood and tone of what is being said as well as the content.

Moving on – the exploratory, information seeking phase continued

You may wish to draw out something extra from the parent on a particular matter, for example by using 'perhaps', 'maybe', 'I wonder if', 'I am wondering whether', 'could it be that?'. This can help achieve greater understanding, for example: 'Perhaps you are saying something about Sam not having any brothers or sisters to negotiate with at home, which makes sharing with his new friends at nursery more difficult for him?' It is worth remembering how often as professionals we ask a whole series of questions and this can make such a conversation seem like a formal interview. In fact, the attuned responses and observations practitioners use in their work with children every day may mean the development of this skill will come quite naturally. Do not be worried about expressing your wish to understand more fully about something you have not fully grasped. It is perfectly all right and appropriate to say out loud: 'I would really like to understand some more about why you think Sam is able to share with his older cousin when they are playing.' Asking open questions promotes enquiry. Open, general questions are helpful at this point in the meeting. They help to build upon the rapport and allow the parent to make choices about what she wants to talk about. Too many direct questions restrict choices. The meeting may then become more about what is only your area of concern. If your questions are sequential and considered, you will encourage richer and better-quality information. Closed questions, on the other hand, can feel intimidating and inquisitive.

Beginning to focus on the purpose of the session

Reflective responses, clarification and summarising gather together key themes and points discussed, move the process along and offer further structure to the interview. It may also be helpful to summarise, so that the conversation stays on track. You can tease out which topic should take priority when several issues are competing for attention. Returning again to asking open questions will foster the sense of working together rather than closing down new possibilities. Approximately halfway through the interview it may be helpful to ask what is often referred to in solution focused therapy as the 'miracle question' (O'Connell 1998).

For example: 'If you woke up tomorrow morning and this problem was solved for Sam, how would you know? What would be different? What would you and others notice?' Once these questions have been answered it is possible to agree the next steps and decide together on ways forward. It is helpful at this point to state some of the successes of the child currently. Deciding what might be an appropriate target or challenge will probably emerge at this stage. Once this is agreed, it is important to be careful that the progress hoped for is going to be over a realistic period of time. In the case of Sam, we might summarise the key points and put the next steps in writing, i.e the strategies to support progress, an agreed time span, and a review date to monitor progress.

The verbal summary of the conversation might agree that Sam will have two friends back to tea before the next meeting. Staff might suggest that the parent will play a simple board game with the children during that visit which involves taking turns. At the pre-school, staff might set up a sharing table where in pairs children can practise their sharing skills daily through games. Sam might be invited to choose a friend and participate in such an activity daily. In the summary, it is also possible to share any other ideas which might be introduced for others in the setting, such as some small-group work with puppets. Other children as well might benefit by being able to join in with these ideas and problem solve together in the area of sharing and taking turns. It would be useful to write the three key strategies down and explain what you might hope to see which will show he is achieving his target, e.g. a reduction in the number of upsetting outbursts Sam has across a week. Being calmer when he is sharing with others might signal things are changing for the better for Sam. The principles of this approach underlie many professional conversations and hopefully you can see how the core skills used explore effectively how together staff and parents can achieve meaningful goals for children.

Using the framework for an initial meeting

In order to reinforce this approach further, below is another example of how staff might use this framework in an initial meeting between a key person and a parent prior to a child starting in the nursery. The different phases and main principles in the conversation will be highlighted in the text as the interview unfolds.

Key person: Now we have had a look around the nursery and done all the required paperwork we have 30 minutes together. It's a chance to share any worries you might have about Izzy's first day. I hope that by the end of our conversation I will have a clearer idea of how together we can help Izzy feel safe and secure and develop a genuine bond together in these first few weeks. I wonder what you are hoping to get from this meeting? (**Negotiating the aim of the conversation.**)

Parent/carer: This is a big step for me, leaving Izzy and returning to work. I need to know that Izzy is being cared for well. If she was unhappy, I am unsure about what is going to help me feel confident as I have not done this before. I would like to know how best to communicate with you about any worries I might have, however silly they may seem. I know too from experience that Izzy cries a lot when we are separated and so I am really worried about how I am going to manage the first morning.

Key person: So at the end of our time together this morning, you would hope to have a clear idea of how we can prepare for the first morning and how we might manage the separation together in a way which will benefit Izzy. You want to know, too, how we will keep the communication going on a daily basis and if I will be available to answer any questions or worries you may have, however trivial they may seem. **(Listening, observing and paraphrasing.)**

Parent/carer: Yes, I would hate it if I was being told everything was fine just as a way of reassuring me when actually Izzy was crying every day.

Key person: I would find it helpful to know a little more about what happens when you leave Izzy with other people and what helps to make these partings easier for both you and Izzy? **(The exploratory, information seeking phase continued.)**

Parent/carer: Well, it is usually OK if I am leaving her with my partner, or her grandmother, but if it is any other member of my extended family, she can become very tearful. I know it can take anything up to an hour to settle her to play. She has a favourite soft piece of material, and once when I had to leave her overnight with my mother I made a recording of myself singing her favourite lullaby which could be played as she went off to sleep.

Key person: It seems as though you are uncertain whether Izzy is going to be able to build the kind of secure relationship with me that she has with her father and grandmother. You are worried she may be unsettled with me, like she is with others she does not know so well. Well, we would encourage you to bring in the things that are important to her and we can certainly play the lullaby at her sleep times. It is possible for us to make a couple of home visits too, so Izzy gets to know me in her home. You may also wish to stay for a while on the first few visits and leave when you feel Izzy is happy. Shall we plan together how, with all those things in place, we might manage the first morning together in a way which will be reassuring for you? **(Reflective responses, clarification and summarising.)** If you woke up tomorrow and you felt less anxious about the things you spoke about at the beginning of this conversation, what would be different? What would you notice about yourself and Izzy? How would you be able to tell that Izzy was settling? **(The miracle question.)**

Parent/carer: Well, I would see myself walking here on the first morning knowing we had talked about everything together. I would be confident that we were clear about how we would handle the goodbye and confident that you would take photographs over the day of Izzy settled and happy. I would also know that you were not suddenly going to suggest I slip away when Izzy was not looking. I know now you would encourage me to take Izzy in my arms and have a proper goodbye cuddle. I would know you would ring at work to tell me how things are going and share with me at the end of the day the important details of Izzy's day. I know Izzy might be unsettled initially, but somehow knowing she had seen your face in our home would mean you are not a complete stranger. Knowing, too, I can ask any questions and not feel you will think I am fussing or being over-protective makes me feel settled inside. The fact that I can be myself and that my worries will be listened to and taken seriously is great for me as her mum.

Key person: So shall we plan the actual hand over on the first morning, what you would like me to do to help you and Izzy say goodbye to each other? Then maybe we can write down some of the key points, which will include the helping ideas, and then set ourselves a goal which we can review together in two weeks. Perhaps we could set ourselves an achievable goal? **(Deciding and planning together/setting a review of progress.)**

Parent/carer: I would like you to feel that you could spend time getting to know Izzy by settling and comforting her and not trying to distract her prematurely and so managing away her understandable distress. It would be good if she had gone into your arms willingly at least once by the end of the second week.

Hopefully the above conversation gives you a sense of how we can begin successfully to cover a number of worries in an initial meeting and meet the needs of both the child and the adult. This will then serve as a foundation upon which to build future meetings. Open dialogue as suggested in this chapter will 'help the mother or father feel reasonably confident that they have made the right decision in placing their baby or child in a particular setting. It will reassure them that their child will be well looked after by mainly one person who will help them to keep in touch with their child' (Elfer, Goldschmied and Selleck 2011, p. 35).

Being creative with the process as a whole staff team

Sometimes it might be possible for staff to think about additional ways in which they could develop this approach in their setting. Creating visual posters can help to demonstrate the setting's commitment to actively seeking the Parent's Voice. Recording any feedback from parental interviews via inviting comments on 'post-its' displayed in the entrance hall makes the process transparent and draws further interest. Providing creche facilities for the younger siblings of the child to be discussed may be helpful. Using staff training opportunities and CPD sessions as an opportunity to practise the approach with colleagues helps staff confidence. Filming each other conducting parent conversations and having supportive dialogues between staff about what is observed is a good team building exercise. It is possible to extend professional buddy systems already in place to encourage more experienced staff to support less experienced staff in developing the core skills required. Staff can also share together any concerns as they arise. Producing an attractive visual cue card for parents to have with them, which highlights the different stages of the conversation/meeting, may also prove helpful to parents with additional language needs or learning disabilities. Visual stimuli like diagrams or visual cues are a powerful form of communication and may help some parents follow the meeting. By confidently using a framework similar to the one above, each of the participants leaves the meeting with a clear idea of its purpose, values the encounter, and feels that the key issues have been tackled in a sympathetic and thoughtful manner.

Protecting spaces to think together

If you focus on parents in this way you are taking a possible first step to developing shared understanding, even if there is a different way of seeing things. Parents may feel they are being heard from *inside* the setting, rather than that they are talking *across* the doorway to staff! Both parties may begin to see themselves as active participants in any change in their child. You may be surprised by how quickly parents are able to express their views and feelings, some of which they may not have expressed before. Protecting spaces to think together which work to a safe framework can allow difficult issues to be communicated safely. Setting aside time to build relationships together in the setting allows parents and professionals to work together more directly and so deal with actual issues which might otherwise create potential difficulty. A series of such conversations may prove to be hopeful as you find a more satisfactory way of evaluating the care given in terms of the experience of the family.

CHAPTER 7

Delighting in the parents and carers of pre-school children at points of transition

At key points of transition in our lives as adults we may feel and communicate both excitement and insecurity. However much consideration has been given by parents to introducing their infant or toddler to childcare facilities, there may be times when there is a momentary mismatch between the outer and the internal reality of doing so. The outer reality may be that a parent or carer has made a decision to give herself time apart from the child across a day. It may be to encourage her child's opportunities for socialisation. On the other hand, a parent might be returning to work as an important part of her own continuing professional and personal development. In the current financial climate it may be for economic reasons. For some others it may have been a decision made for them for social care reasons and as a result of a child protection issue. Whatever the reason for the choice that informed the decision, it is likely that the inner reality of the decision feels from time to time less clear cut. A variety of emotional responses to the separation may at different times and because of different circumstances temporarily unsettle us.

Likewise, the inner reality for the child in terms of these decisions may mean he is initially unsettled by change or even overwhelmed. We are familiar with children's responses and needs at such a time of change, loss and separation. The 'snuggly' or favourite soft toy which is carried with him across 'the bridge' from home to the setting is one noticeable expression of a child in the process of transition. The 'transitional object' (Winnicott 1971), as it is called, represents the first relationship with a primary carer. It accompanies the child as they 'come into being' and separate from the parent. It is symbolic of the child beginning to establish a relationship with the world. Through the use of such an object, young children are exploring what was 'there and then' and what is 'here and now' and the space between those two places.

Supporting parents at the point of transition

But what about parents at key points of transition in their lives? In some ways they are both looking back and looking forward. We may wonder whether, when they are separating from their children, some experiences of their own childhood are

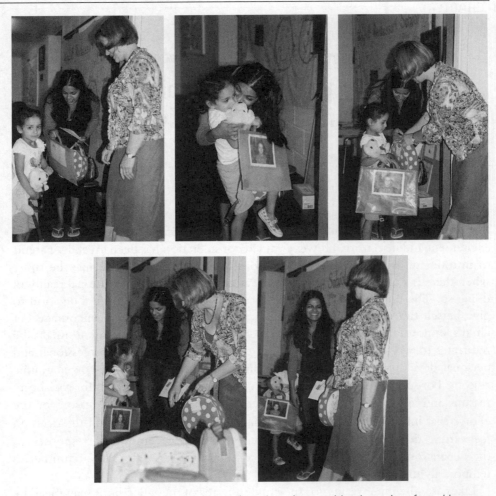

Figure 7.1 *Attentive meeting, greeting and parting: the transition is made safe and happy for both mother and daughter by the nursery teacher.*

awoken. Memories of their own separations may be very alive to them at such times. They may be wondering who is available to them to help them empathically with some of these feelings. They will almost certainly have aspirations for their children and hope they enter safely and confidently into new experiences as they may or may not have done themselves.

> At first it's like a punch in the solar plexus. It's a physical as well as an emotional experience . . . I returned to work when my son was twelve months old. I left him playing happily with his key person who he seemed to really like. I felt confused as I was happy for him and sad for myself. I had a mixture of anxiety and grief inside me and for several weeks I cried as I drove myself to work.
>
> (*A father who had been a main carer*)

Early Years practitioners are experts in 'comings and goings'. Through their highly tuned observational skills, they can become adept at anticipating what might happen next in response to a given situation. This is because they are used to supporting children's needs when they take their next steps in their learning and development. Across each working day in any childcare provision two experiences recur. Firstly, there is loss and separation. Secondly, there is expectation, anticipation and hope associated with coming back together with those you love and who care for you. In fact, we might say that the 'hellos and goodbyes' of a typical nursery or pre-school setting are the stuff of life: a continual process of 'letting go'. For many children and parents this may be a complicated process if the children have spent many hours daily since they were infants in group day childcare. In certain ways staff may become a 'secure base' (Bowlby 1988), and a safe pair of hands for the parents too, as they 'come and go' daily. Practitioners through good, sensitive relationships can become empathic to parents' needs as well. Through building trust and rapport, they also indirectly help support parental confidence and competence in the outside world. It seems important to offer this when parents are separated from their children. Many parents hope that the new adults in their children's lives will be able to reflect on their situation too, offer guidance and help 'organise their feelings' (Cooper *et al.* 1998) by listening to their parental anxieties.

In *Developing Attachments in Early Years Settings* (Read 2009) I discussed the 'Circle of Security' (Cooper *et al.* 1998) and how children demonstrate to adults their caregiving and careseeking needs, and I suggested that parents might also require to have their own attachment needs attended to similarly at points of separation and transition.

> The application of this sensitivity to parental needs and the care given to routine encounters at the doorway of your setting are significant communications in terms of the success you will have in building trust and rapport. How we conduct ourselves in our meetings and greetings, consultations and parent meetings really matters.
>
> (Read 2009, p. 115)

Most parents want and benefit from support. Some parents leaving and returning to their children may hope for and regard as positive experiences:

- Being greeted with smiles and delighted in.
- Receiving help to organise their feelings through accessible and responsive practitioners.
- Regarding the setting as a safe haven from time to time if they feel anxious or overwhelmed.
- Sharing in the celebration of their child's day.
- Hearing simple daily accounts of their child from the adult caring for her who really knows the child.

There is an element of imagined risk, leaving one's child on the first occasion with an unfamiliar adult. Communicating effectively with parents and taking their anxieties seriously strengthens their sense of security. It also helps soothe the imagined risk. How is it possible to do this well? Perhaps by listening to one mother's experience of one phase in her son's life at nursery, and how the behaviour of the staff distanced her, we might discover what was actually needed.

A mother's account

Memhet is 3 years and 6 months old and had been attending his nursery for 2 terms with no problems. He was settled and happy and had formed good attachments with several of the staff. During the Easter Holidays the old building which had housed the nursery was to be demolished to make way for a new Children's Centre, and a temporary building was erected on a nearby site. Upon his return to the temporary building Memhet became upset and anxious about being left. I was encouraged by the staff to leave him crying and I did so on several occasions, only to find that the problem became worse, with him getting very upset at any mention of the nursery. He also became fearful of being alone and going upstairs at home. Memhet's two mornings a week became very stressful experiences for both of us, with him clinging to me and not wanting me to go. The only approach that the pre-school had was for me to leave. 'He'll be OK in 10 minutes', they would tell me. I decided to take some advice from a nursery in a nearby town which had a softer approach to separation anxiety. They advised me to stay with Memhet for an hour, have a happy time playing, and then leave early together. This, they said, would build up a positive experience of the place and gradually would enable me to leave with fewer problems. I approached Memhet's nursery with the plan, and although they agreed to try it 'for a few weeks', they were clearly unhappy about it. They said that he would get used to me being there and I would cause more problems than I would solve. They made me feel neurotic and over-anxious and, as a result, I began to feel resentful and mistrustful of them. As discussed, I stayed with Memhet for the first hour and encouraged him to become engaged in activities. This was difficult as he was very anxious that I would leave and clung to my side. We left together after an hour. While I was at the setting, the staff almost entirely ignored me and their disapproval was quite evident. I stuck to my guns and carried on for the next few weeks and began to see Memhet get more confident and involved in the play. The staff began putting pressure on me to go and do a bit of shopping so I agreed. Memhet became immediately hysterical, but when I got back 30 minutes later I was taken to a window and shown Memhet playing happily. I was told that this is why I must leave. 'Because he's fine once you've gone.' I was unconvinced and felt that he was only fine because he'd had to dig deep and get through it. I was proved right the next morning when we drove to the nursery and Memhet became hysterical before even getting out of the car. I drove home and telephoned the pre-school to say that he was being removed for the rest of the term. When I told them what had happened in the car park, their only suggestion was that one of them come out to the car to get him. The whole experience was very traumatic for us both. I was made to feel completely neurotic and a nuisance by all the staff. At one point, I suggested that they do the relevant checks and I start coming in as a helper but that idea was quickly dismissed. Their only approach to the problem was for me to leave so that eventually he'd get used to it. 'What will you do when he goes to school?', they would ask me. 'You'll have to leave him then.' They admitted that the move to the new building was disruptive and that they were surprised that more of the children hadn't been affected. But they had no plan to deal with the children that were affected. Memhet is returning with his brother in the September term but I have lost a lot of confidence in the staff and feel that my relationship with them is now strained.

So, what may have gone wrong on this occasion?

Most importantly, why was it not possible to delight in this mother during this important transition. What made it so difficult to take in and digest her concerns on behalf of her child? It is not difficult to imagine in our minds the series of encounters between staff and mother during this time. We can probably imagine how we might feel both as the parent and as the practitioner. Certainly the patterns of communication would have lacked vitality, and an absence of empathy would have shown itself through a lack of fluidity of body language, eye contact or voice tone. In short, the encounters would have been stressful for the adults concerned, which would have been communicated to Memhet at some level. In the first chapter of the book the two energies associated with communication, namely love and fear, were discussed, and this mother certainly felt the tangible communication of defensiveness, distrust, narrow-mindedness and even rejection of her offer to become a parent helper, causing distress and hopelessness.

We might speculate that the staff were overwhelmed themselves by the prospect of the move, which may have become task-focused in order to make it more manageable. Had there been losses in the staff team, which were unexpressed? What is it actually like to say goodbye to a cosy homespun environment and step into the 'one-stop' shop of the Children's Centre. Staff may have done a good enough job preparing the majority of the children. On the other hand, the fact that the staff might have seemed overwhelmed due to the additional demands of the move may have had an unconscious effect on the children. Like the children of overwhelmed parents, they may have quickly learned in some cases not to add to the adults' worries and so were 'good' as they did not feel safe enough to express their 'big feelings'. Of course, other children make additional demands on adults at stressful times.

If we were observing this experience and what was being communicated we might summarise it as an expression of some kind of unnamed fear which meant staff had their 'eyes down' and were unable to relate or empathise with the parent. This idea is discussed in Chapter 2, 'What do we mean by communication?' What would we observe if we were 'a fly on the wall' in this setting? We would see disconnection, an 'us and them' mentality, an inability to sustain shared thinking, and a wish to make a complex, uncertain situation simple and easy to solve. We would possibly sense too an inability to tolerate a different point of view.

Blaming and scapegoating the parent as 'neurotic and over-anxious'

We know that very often when we are in survival mode we can become defensive. One way of dealing with difficult situations is to be of 'one mind' on a matter. It feels better if we let one person be different because it makes us feel better when we are feeling vulnerable. To put a problem or problems into another person often happens when we are unable to ask for help ourselves and when we are surviving a difficult experience. It just seems too difficult to connect with people in the here and now. Interestingly, this can happen when we have suffered a loss and feel overwhelmed by the demands of the change. People who have lost something will regress temporarily and this is when dialogue is replaced by 'scapegoating'. We do not do this intentionally, but 'cutting off' can help us deal with stress and change. We cannot be at our best all the time. However, when we 'lose' a parent, or a child is temporarily withdrawn as in this case, it is important to be curious and reflective.

Respecting parents' expertise in their own lives

The situation we have been exploring is not an unfamiliar experience. It is therefore worth thinking about in some detail. What is clear is that there is an inability to delight in this mother as the most significant person in her child's life. She is the centre of her child's world and yet her insight is seemingly not fully acknowledged. There seems to be a collision of philosophies between the staff and the family. Instead of the heart and head working together, something has split apart. Good communication has broken down and finding a bridge back to working in partnership looks unlikely. What is perhaps surprising about this experience is that there was almost certainly a shared goal for all the adults involved. We might imagine that goal was a settled and happy child who should be free of anxiety to play and learn. Reaching out and continuing to engage with this mother has been temporarily lost. What is so puzzling is that there are no unreasonable requests being made. In Chapter 2, communication is described as a 'two-way exchange that involves information and emotion'. We have also noted 'the extra dimension in your relationship that makes it very powerful and important. You are by and large talking about the parent's child.' Central to developing good communication is the building up of trust. It is clear that the energy for good communication has faltered. In fact, at the point of a significant transition, i.e. leaving the former nursery 'home' and moving to a new 'home', there is a breakdown in the partnership. The parent is quite literally left desolate and isolated like the demolished building!

Communications which allow for compassion, warmth and commitment

Looking through the eyes of the child

On one hand we might say the former nursery building is just a building, but through the eyes of a child it may be much more. It might be a collection of atmospheres, smells, tastes, tactile memories, favourite corners, patterns on curtains transfused by sunlight and familiar sounds. It may be the place where 'I spilt some red paint' or the crack in the floorboards where 'I poured sand and chalk dust'. Important places like this are also psychological spaces and become part of a child's dream life and internal world. They are safe havens and secure places to explore, to be, and to feel spiritually at home in the absence of a primary caregiver. Each child explores this space in her own unique way and saying goodbye to it will evoke a unique response. It may bring excitement, anxiety or sadness. Can children mourn? Bowlby thought so. Acknowledging losses can bring about the possibility of continuing with new experiences. However, if Memhet's transition was experienced as difficult and left inadequately addressed, it might become a traumatic memory. This needs to be taken seriously and thought about. On this occasion it was not possible to think together about Memhet's feelings. This left the mother alone to make a decision about how to re–establish her son's security.

Saying goodbye to a building matters

How can we best help a child say goodbye to such a special environment? How might the adults communicate that they value a child's experience of change? In the lead up to a significant change, it is helpful to talk to children generally about how change is a natural part of life and that nothing stays the same for very long. This might be done through talking about the transformational cycle of the seasons and introducing nature studies, e.g. the lifecycle of the frog. 'Changes' is a key theme in the SEAL (Social and Emotional Aspects of Learning) National Strategy which provides a reading list for books that are suitable to read to children from the Foundation Stage to KS2 and upwards. Involving children in taking photographs of the old building and setting them alongside images of the new building for comparison, as 'same and different', is another possible activity which works at a symbolic level as well. Involving the children in moving a few small, manageable objects into the 'new home' rather than them returning to everything having been done in their absence is another possibility. We only have to consider the thought we put into our children when we move house. Professional closeness and respect between the parents and the staff at these times adds to their security.

Looking through the eyes of the parent

Good communication between parents and their childcare provision is importantly associated with outcomes for children. Feeling valued as the first and most enduring educator of one's child is a good starting point for trusting that your unique knowledge and finely tuned observations of your own child's emotional development are important to others. Believing that one's informed intuition and common sense, as a competent parent, can be shared is essential. This particular mother has had a good experience of care herself as a child and intuitively feels it is appropriate to take her child's distress seriously. Parents are actively invited to make a contribution to and be included in all observational assessment. Any system for helping practitioners get to know and understand children must include and value contributions from parents and carers.

A parent senses whether she is seen as an individual or merely reduced to being 'Memhet's Mum'. Being 'met as a person' (McCluskey 2005) means staff have empathy for painful feelings during goodbyes and will not try to smooth things over prematurely with a standard response such as 'he'll be fine'. A 'whole family' plan which is mutually agreed and which focuses on the child's needs is about reaching out and genuinely engaging. Staff who are reflective about how children express what they might be feeling in the moment are tuned in. If children are not developmentally able to find words for the emotional experience, then it is the job of the adults to think and feel on behalf of the child. Respecting and recognising the good intentions of parents is about mutuality. 'Concentrating on the good intentions of parents helps to give them a positive self-image. Just as children need positive images reflected about themselves, so do parents. The attitude of the staff must therefore be to show parents respect' (Bruce, Meggitt and Grenier 2010, p. 509). When possible and appropriate, the child's voice should be sought.

Looking through the eyes of the practitioner

It is interesting to consider how we might apply the disposition recommended for conducting observations in a setting to the situation described.

> To be a good observer . . . requires a space in the mind where thoughts can begin to take shape and where confused experiences can be held in an inchoate form until meaning becomes clearer. This kind of mental activity requires a capacity to tolerate anxiety, uncertainty, discomfort, helplessness, a sense of bombardment.
>
> (Rustin 1989, pp. 20–2)

It is the aim of all practitioners working with young children in their care to enhance their sense of security, otherwise their capacity to explore and play is diminished. When we are thoroughly engaged we reach 'a state of joy, creativity and total involvement' (Laevers 2000 cited in Fawcett 2009, p. 94). This is often described as 'flow'. An anxious child does not enjoy this satisfaction or sense of well-being.

What do practitioners require to 'flow' in their communications?

We return to finding 'spaces to think' about what is happening as a whole staff team. This involves looking beyond the move as a task and paying attention to one's feelings. Trusting and listening to what the staff are feeling before and after the move is important information. 'Getting your head down and getting through' may mirror the way the children feel they have to deal with the event. Incorporating into your planning some meaningful activities and incorporating the children's ideas can make the move fun and interesting. Transferring the principles of your daily observation to a child's emotional life could lead to staff asking some interesting questions such as:

- What lies behind this child's behaviour?
- Can I look at this from a different perspective?
- What are the many possibilities in this situation?
- How can I work with the parent to decide on next steps and solve the 'problem'?

To have anticipated that each child will have a unique response to change and recognising signs of vulnerability can be a real strength. It reminds us of our humanity, which offers us an opportunity to connect with others at times of upheaval. Welcoming parental feedback on the move is like having a fresh pair of eyes in the setting, and is cheaper than employing an outside consultant! Hopefully, all of the above suggestions are reasonable and within the scope of each person involved to achieve.

Where does the solution lie?

The solution lies in the two wonderful offers of help from the mother: firstly, in the patient endeavour of this parent to gradually build up Memhet's confidence day by day through extended play in the setting; secondly, in the offer of becoming a parent helper.

There is compassion too for the practitioners who were not offered support, space, or time to step back and use their emotional intelligence in the ways they would have wished to have done.

Earlier in this book we explored, through the ideas implicit in Transactional Analysis, how we function as three people in one: a child, a parent and an adult. Similarly, many for us working in the Public Sector today, faced with continuous change, vacillate between certainty and a sense of insecurity. We function within the organisations we work in at times as a child or a parent and at other times as an adult. Someone demanding change and the need to modernise can be experienced as an over-demanding parent. If those managing our Services are not attuned to staff needs, then change can awaken old ways of functioning in order to cope. Staff may feel they have to grow up before their time, become an adult and not ask for what they really need or show dependency. What did this staff group need from their senior managers, I wonder? Unlike Memhet, they were unable to say that this was too much change, too soon, in too short a time. Instead they had to present a false self, coping and compliant. Senior managers have to be understanding parents too, and allow for uncertainty, regression and anxiety within their staff teams when there is significant change and loss.

Supervision as a 'thinking space'

On a final note, the reader may wonder what a 'thinking space' as referred to in the earlier part of the chapter actually means. Or how we can incorporate it into our professional lives. We have seen how, when we feel vulnerable, we can wrap a layer of protection around us. It is possible that at such times an offer of help may be experienced with suspicion. One example of a professional context in which to think aloud about these tricky responses to stress is Supervision. Supervision is an opportunity for each practitioner (supervisee) to bring his thoughts and feelings about a key group of children to an experienced professional colleague (supervisor) and for both parties to have a reflective conversation about chosen issues and situations.

> Supervision can be a very important part of taking care of one's self, staying open to new learning: and an indispensible part of the helper's well being, on-going self development, self awareness and commitment to development. We think that lack of supervision can contribute to feelings of staleness, rigidity and defensiveness.
>
> (Hawkins and Shohet 2006, p. 5)

For practitioners, the process of supervision offers an opportunity to rely on a space where they can share the demands of being a key person, and makes the possibility of meeting their key children's needs. Staff can also share their disappointments, struggles and inter-staff tensions. Would it have helped in this case, I wonder?

CHAPTER 8

Empathy and communication

Two individuals, conversing honestly, can be inspired by the feeling that they are engaged in a joint enterprise, aiming at inventing an art of living together which has not been tried before.

(Zeldin 1998, p. 31)

What happens in a meaningful encounter with another person can quite simply change oneself. In this chapter we will develop further some of the ideas described in Chapter 3 about the importance of communicating with parents and understand how vital it is to be able 'to walk in someone else's shoes'. By paying attention and monitoring our own choice of language and our body language during parental conversations, we can give parents an authentic experience of being thought about and cared about as people. Those of us who have been on the receiving end of a communication which has felt as though we were not being listened to understand how it can feel, as if one has been missed as a person. Empathy prevents the chance of misunderstandings and miscommunications. This is because our focus is always going to be on the other person and noticing how what we communicate is received.

Often what we feel about the person who asks us to do something has a more powerful impact on us than what they might say or do. The way we are asked to do something also affects whether we do it or not. Experiments have shown that we prefer faces which resemble our own. There is a lot going on when we are face to face with someone! It is therefore worth investing in face to face encounters. Building a relationship with someone and engaging her in a conversation involves being patient, calm and confident. Developing an empathic interpersonal way of being requires thought.

It is worth thinking about occasions in your life when you have had memorable, helpful encounters. Perhaps you had really lost your temper or were very distressed about something. If you sought help from someone in this situation and felt you were really helped by him, go back and remember that time. What was it about the person who helped you? Try to remember what qualities he brought to the interaction. How did he stand or sit with you? What did you feel when you looked into his face? By thinking again about your experiences, you have, I hope, found within you an invaluable resource. What you received, you can now use in the service of others. This is like the babies in your care who have had their needs 'imagined' by their parents through empathy. These babies will become the toddlers and young children who show care when somebody falls over in the garden and may even verbalise: 'I think Ahdaf has hurt herself.'

Empathy in the workplace

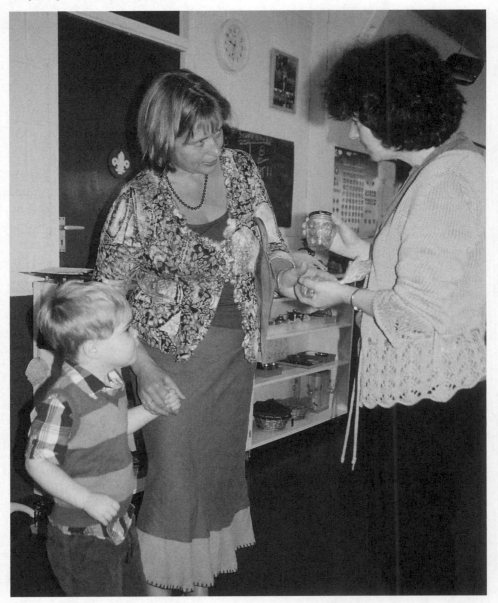

Figure 8.1 *The nursery manager shares with this boy's key person the items he has brought in a jar. He watches with trust and interest.*

Participants on the workshops we run often speak of the occasions when they feel they have not had good enough empathic experiences at work. It is not unusual for practitioners to talk about managers who do not seem to be able to understand that their work is often emotionally demanding. The consequence of this is that the challenges placed upon them daily sometimes leave them feeling overwhelmed.

Likewise, many of them have had experiences with parents who do not seem interested in working in partnership with them. They may have given considerable thought to setting appropriate challenges for their children. They may have spent time creatively recording their children's progress and next steps by taking great personal pride in completing their Learning Journeys. This sometimes involves spending their own spare time preparing folders and displaying work. However, they meet parents who do not seem to understand the commitment involved in such a process. Dismissing or seeming to ignore staff's efforts in this way affects their own sense of internal security as professional people. A parent's capacity to appreciate and understand accurately how every effort, however small, is an important contribution by a practitioner matters to her. At the heart of such a commitment is their children's long-term well-being, mental health and educational attainment. Working together is an important part of forging common interests, concerns and goals. When children are at the heart of any communication, we need to give our full attention to these aims. When we remember that just as the 'internal pot of gold' (Baron-Cohen 2011) we create inside a child by filling him up with positive emotions has a similar effect on our sense of our self in our professional lives, we become aware of how important it is that our empathy is alive and kicking!

Colleague empathy

On the other hand, colleagues also share when they have been struggling personally and professionally. Very often the positive relationships in their setting have supported them and made them feel valued. The importance of consistent, friendly and confident professional relationships has a considerable impact on the well-being of staff in general. It is clear that small acts of empathy like being a wonderful listener and appreciating colleagues' feelings contribute to the emotional climate of the setting. Recently, one workshop participant sitting next to a colleague from the same pre-school turned to her and said: 'It means so much when you sense that I am at the end of my resources, like the other day when you helped me out in the afternoon session with Tommy when he was crying so much.' This very warm acknowledgement led on to others sharing their experiences of professional bonds. When somebody sensitively responds to us we feel understood and the psychological distance closes. This skill which involves staying with, and naming, the experience is about being in a relationship with another in a way which does not avoid unsettled feelings but engages with her. It is not enough just to identify the feelings of another person; it is important to know how to make an appropriate emotional response. In other words, just as sustained empathy between a carer and a baby will result in a sense of high self-esteem in the developing infant, so it is true for adult to adult relationships. One can feel revitalised by satisfactory encounters – whereas when another person is unable to empathise with us we may be left with low self-worth.

What are conversations like in your setting when colleagues require support from the team? Can you remember an occasion when you felt you were focusing more on your own thoughts than on the person you were supposed to be listening to? How quick are you at picking up on the discomfort of others? When was the last time somebody thanked you because you had been good at understanding his feelings? Do you ever think about how you can improve your skills and become more intuitive about what people are not actually saying?

What is empathy?

Empathy is 'being able to understand accurately the other person's position, to identify with "where they are at". It means being able to find solutions to what might otherwise be a deadlock between incompatible goals. Empathy makes the other person feel valued, enabling them to feel their thoughts and feelings have been heard, acknowledged and respected' (Baron-Cohen 2011, p. 12). Empathy begins within the context of a warm loving relationship. Let's remember how in Attachment terms this happens. This will help us see how reflective, empathic communication between adults may help develop secure, trustworthy professional relationships as well.

Attachment and empathy

The first relationship which develops between a primary caregiver and the infant seeking connection to another involves the parents' tone of voice, and ways of looking and smiling at the infant. By responding in this way to the baby, he sees himself as loveable. Whatever the baby offers, be it feelings, actions, gestures or sounds, is taken up and given back by the parent. We can imagine how this reflecting back affects the child's view of himself and his self-esteem. An attuned parent, delighting in an infant, intuitively adjusts what is offered so that it comes back to the baby in a lovable form. This important way of being in a sort of 'dance' together grows and develops. For example, a hungry crying toddler in a high chair whose carer responds with a tuned-in, rhythmical, empathic response such as 'I know you're really hungry, it's coming, it's coming, sweetie-pie' gives the baby something to chew on emotionally and helps him manage the brief wait (which may feel like a lifetime to him!) before his physical hunger is fully satisfied.

It is so encouraging to feel that setting the correct tempo when we are meeting and greeting parents can provide a similar mirroring function, e.g. 'Hello, don't worry about that, let me hold the changing bag while you give Tom a lovely hug goodbye.' In this way we confirm and strengthen the more positive aspects of the adult and reflect back a genuine appreciation of her as a resilient individual. In Chapter 7 we explored how alienating it feels for a caring parent to be seen in the eyes of others as a 'kind of mother' she does not recognise herself to be. The process of tuning in to another is a combination of empathy and informed intuition. Informed intuition is based upon being both knowledgeable and experienced, and being curious about why we and others do things in particular ways. This leads us to develop eventually, with language, a capacity to explain and share with others an understanding of ourselves and others.

We can begin to explore the quality of this experience by returning to the principles of Attachment thinking and remember the baby at birth seeking care from his mother. A baby seeks eye contact within minutes of entering the world. A baby's growth of connection to its carer involves touch and tone of voice, and leads on to being able to imagine or 'mentalize' (Fonargy 2001) her caregiver's mind.

'Responsiveness and attunement' (Stern 1991) are the necessary key characteristics of practitioners in supporting children's emotional learning. It is through rapid, regulated, face to face interactions that the attuned caregiver not only minimises the infant's negative feelings but also maximises his positive affective states (Schore 2001). 'Young children are very dependent on adults for comfort. They need to spend a lot of time being held, rocked and gently stroked as they experience their physical feelings with great intensity. For an infant the intensity of their feelings gives rise to their first feelings of anxiety' (Manning-Morton 2003, p. 31). It is perhaps fair to say that our needs as adults at times, when overwhelmed by anxiety, are not dissimilar to an infant. We require, too:

- The presence of another who offers containment and comfort.
- Help to regulate our emotional state.
- An empathic relationship to offer 'relief and satisfaction' (McCluskey 2005).
- Help to restore hope.

We develop empathy through experiencing it

You cannot teach empathy. This would mean dispassionately trying to second guess and calculate what someone is thinking. Empathy involves feeling and is something shared. We cannot tell people to be caring towards each other and expect it will happen automatically. It requires time and patience to understand others and by so doing we demonstrate empathy in action. This in turn allows others to go on and re-create reciprocity in their relationships. Having the capacity to begin to experience this through close continuous relationships with children gives us a map for our professional relationships with adults too, and the significance not simply of what we say, but of how we relate to them and how we say it (Brazelton, Berry and Greenspan 2000).

Professional attachment relationships with parents

Let us bridge between the mother–infant experience and the mother–practitioner experience and see how this reciprocal communication or 'heart beat of human existence' (Kaplan 1995) might translate in small but significant encounters in pre-school settings.

Imagine that a mother enters a nursery with a crying baby, looking dishevelled and overwhelmed. She expresses her concern that the baby in her arms is going to be even more distressed when she leaves. Her arms are full, as is her mind with the impending separation.

What is required at this moment in order for this mother to leave in a different state from that in which she arrived? How might the staff in your setting start a conversation with this parent? What response would you hope to receive if you were this parent? Key to a positive outcome in this scenario is how the practitioner responds in terms of body language, tone of voice, facial expression and eye contact.

Body language: Our body language expresses how we really feel. How we lean forward and adjust the angle of our head to a listening mode has an important impact. It conveys how much we are concentrating. However, being too close in such a posture may feel invasive and too dominant. Gentle, intermittent nodding of the head can indicate that we have some understanding of what is being said. Yet the pace, rhythm and timing of such interactions alter the message. Equally, our posture reveals how open we are. If we are tense and stressed and preoccupied with other work issues, the parent will sense there are other things going on below the surface. Sensing this may limit the demands that are placed on the practitioner. We may employ this way of being to keep people at arm's length!

Tone of voice: The rate at which we speak and the pitch of our voice can have a significant impact on the mood and calmness of the encounter. It indicates how grounded and empathic we are to events. When we speak with an energised voice rather than a flatness of tone, we are better able to match any anger we meet. We are able to respond with an energetic response such as 'I can see that is really upsetting for you at the moment.' At the same time, keeping an eye on the modulation of our voice can result in our responses having a soothing effect, too.

Facial expression: Facial expressions give us clues as to the emotional weather inside someone. Faces on the whole have a fluidity and mobility which in the lower face are sculpted by the muscles around the mouth and jaw and convey levels of tension to the onlooker. The facial expressions we see mirrored back at us also guide us as to the kind of message we have conveyed. In other words the facial expressions we see may have a mirroring effect. It reminds us of the baby who searches the mother's face and sees a reflection of him or herself.

Eye contact: We may have heard of the observation that a certain person smiles with his eyes. The intensity of eye contact, avoidance of eye contact and steadiness of gaze all contribute to the overall emotional atmosphere that is created. Research has shown that peacekeeping forces in Iraq 'whose members wear sunglasses, report higher incidence of unrest, and incur more casualties, than those whose members keep their eyes visible' (Dutton 2010, p. 71). To return to the idea of the face as a mirror, we can see how, just as a baby's vitality is altered by mutual reinforcement, 'The mother is affirmed in her sense of herself as a "good" mother by her baby's smiles of recognition; the baby we may suppose, feels affirmed in his state of being by the mother's lively and smiling response to him' (Wright 1991, p. 12), and therefore adults in face to face contact may enjoy a similar good feeling. These skills are further developed in Chapter 3. However, for now we shall return to our overwhelmed mother arriving at the nursery one morning.

Offering an overwhelmed mother a sensitive response in a supportive environment

Step 1: To give a reassuring smile upon first meeting.

Step 2: To acknowledge verbally and empathically what you see: 'You look really weighed down with both the baby and all her things. Let me take the nappy bag and her feeding bottles.'

Step 3: To offer an emotional responsive solution which appeals to the higher brain function, which may be: 'It would be a lovely start to the day for Amy and yourself and help with the goodbye if you gave her a hug and kiss.'

Step 4: To speak to the baby in warm, confident, rhythmical tones, which indicate there is a change coming up: 'Are you ready to come to me now so we can wave goodbye to mummy?'

Step 5: To comfort the baby, give him a favourite soft toy and speak softly to him.

Step 6: To offer reassuring dialogue in the same tone of voice across to the mother, offering her a phone call later, some photos of her child in a settled state and the reassurance that his crying at separation is appropriate.

Establishing this culture of respect and routine is very containing for both mother and baby. However, perhaps we might consider honestly how we do at times respond in the presence of someone who is overwhelmed: how we help manage the helplessness it may arouse in us! It might not be unusual to ask a lot of questions in order to fill the space between yourself and the other person, e.g. 'Do you have her changing bag? Has she had her breakfast?' We may reveal by the tone of our voice, speed of words and quick bodily movements a level of impatience and a wish to get the handover done as quickly as possible. An unintentionally brusque 'Give her to me and you go' might even escape your lips. We may even share our frustration with colleagues about how yet another day has started in this way. We might refer to the mother as 'She' and feel that we have no real part in supporting change for this parent. The parent becomes labelled as 'the one who always . . .', and letting our frustration out in these ways gives temporary relief from the situation but is ultimately unsatisfactory.

Young first-time mothers

Figure 8.2 *The nursery has created a safe space for mothers to chat with each other and share experiences.*

When asked about her experience of being a single mother, one young woman spoke of the conflicting messages and communications she had received from the professionals around her. Her first experience, like most people, was with the maternity services. She had been surprised by how much easier she found it to share her fears and anxieties with a male midwife who would sit and listen to her. On the other hand, she found herself being told 'Come along, you've got a child now, pick yourself up' by the female midwives. Could it be that the 'sitting down' of the male midwife was the most powerful action in this situation? Quite literally 'getting alongside someone' has a powerful impact. We know how the height of a chair in an interview affects whether we feel we are being talked down to or not. How do you imagine the other response was delivered? The briskness of tone leads one to imagine it was given from a standing position or on the move in a busy fashion. How different to be able to say from a position of mutuality: 'I am sure you feel very tired right now as you have just given birth to your beautiful baby. We will help you get back on your feet. I wonder if there is a first step we might manage together right now?'

Having been on the receiving end of such a 'jollying along', this young woman found it hard to ask questions for fear she would be thought of as stupid. This first interface with health professionals has left her assuming she will meet a similar response from other professionals. Now she leaves her son's nursery feeling unable to ask questions, too. Recently her son seems to have become clingy and tearful and she is told to leave, as she is making 'it' worse. Her overwhelming sense is that she is in the way, that the staff have 'seen it all before', and their briskness signals they want her to go so they can get on with the routine. She has been told that it is not that he does not like it there, but of course he would rather be with her, and that he will forget about her as soon as she is gone and be fine. As she leaves she feels she is part of the problem and guilty for making her son have these feelings. She says it is often difficult to get on with the day after such a parting. What lost opportunity has occurred for developing a parental relationship in this situation?

Nurturing parents

There is a real tangle of confused communications for this mother to unravel alone. This description is not dissimilar to the one in the earlier chapter. However, many new, young mothers can feel very easily de-skilled when professionals are so certain about the solution. There is a real psychological distance in such an interaction and no sense of wishing to personalise the response. Perhaps this is what the mother describes as 'they have seen it all before', i.e. you are the same as everybody else. The question that is perhaps unspoken for this mother is: 'If my feelings can be dismissed in this way, is that also true for my child when he tries to express his unmet needs?'

If we look at the Principles of the EYFS – unique child (parent), positive relationships, enabling environment, learning and development – we could equally apply these to our work with parents. Supporting our parents to support their children has been an overall goal since the Green Paper 'Every Child Matters' (2003), and the most recent 'Five-a-day' campaign (2011) is aimed at improving parents knowledge of child development and nurture. Generally, we have moved away from regarding the caregivers as the problem for problematic behaviour in their children – although currently popular views of the causes of the recent 'riots' are testing this viewpoint dramatically. On the whole, we wish to find ways of changing patterns of behaviour, to give messages such as 'all parents struggle' and to celebrate positive resources in the individual parent. A professional's role in this commitment is to 'be bigger, stronger, wiser and kinder' (Cooper *et al.* 1998). These qualities of empathy, responsiveness and good attachments inform our role as a citizen within a community, too.

In her article 'Attachment: supporting young children's emotional well-being' (2007), Juliet Neil-Hall identifies the ten key emotional needs that all human beings have: attention, acceptance, appreciation, encouragement, affection, respect, support, comfort, approval, security. Fulfilment of these key emotional needs was absent during our young mother's interface with some of the professional services. It can be a good training exercise to think with colleagues about how these needs might have been met more effectively. More adventurous training opportunities could include role playing and filming such a scenario and discussing your observations as a staff team. A whole-team approach to the support required can then be agreed and implemented as a protocol or statement of intent when working with parents in your setting. The intuitive, empathic gifts practitioners have for being in relationship with children make us hopeful that the seeds of good parental relationships are flourishing in most Early Years settings and that the wider educational system has much to learn from such good practice.

In the light of the current challenges in our society with regard to re-establishing trust between all of us and rebuilding communication and empathy in communities, this chapter ends with a few lines from a poem:

> So hope for a great sea-change
> On the far side of revenge.
> Believe that a further shore
> Is reachable from here.
> Believe in miracles
> And cures and healing wells.
>
> From Seamus Heaney's *The Cure of Troy* (1990)

Heaney's sea change is clearly heard in Mary Gordon's timely clarion call to develop our professional emotional empathy in relation to others through reflection, the 'fourth R' of Education:

> It is not enough to *know* that the sustained and loving engagement of parents is the single most influential factor on the healthy growth of the human child and if that knowledge is not acted on – if we continue to leave parents, especially the most vulnerable of them, to struggle alone without the support and resources they need to give to their child a healthy start in life. We have to stop the rhetoric and do the things that *will* put children first. We need to honor parents and recognise the interdependence between family-friendly societies, competent parenting, and healthy, confident children.
>
> (Gordon 2009, pp. 221–2)

CHAPTER 9

Dealing with difficulty

It's not the differences that divide us. It's our judgements about each other that do.

(Margaret Wheatley 2002)

It is inevitable that those working with people will come up against difficulties. There are always the possibilities for misunderstanding, disappointment, frustration and irritation because we live our lives amongst others but no one sees the world exactly as we do.

However, curiosity is a great help in maintaining and restoring goodwill by allowing others to tell their story. It is always easier to tell our story (our side of things) when we feel that others are genuinely curious about us. Curiosity helps us to be more attentive and less judgemental. An example could be when you are making a relationship with a family from a different culture from your own. The more you show an interest in and ask questions about this family's life in a sensitive and attentive way, the easier it will be for the family to share their information and for a bridge of understanding and acceptance to emerge. This allows for a much easier transition for the baby or child to move between the two worlds across this bridge.

Nevertheless, when you choose to work in the education and care of young children, the possibility for difficulties to arise multiplies when you are working with their parents. This is because you are not only working within the constraints of laws of the land and the policies of your setting, and under the management of your leaders, you are also working with the most precious things in your clients' lives: their children. This has been said before and needs to be remembered again.

Over the many years that the authors have worked with practitioners, teachers and families, we have come across many stories when it comes to dealing with difficulty. Whilst every situation is unique, there are similarities that link other people's stories with your own experience. It is hoped that the following stories will give you some reassurance and guidance in your own encounters with difficulty.

Biting and other behavioural problems

It is common that when a child does not have sufficient language skills or the social and emotional skills of turn taking, waiting or seeking help, he will resort to biting or pinching as an effective means of getting what he wants. It is alarming because it is sudden and aggressive and triggers adult revulsion because of its bestiality. Whilst you, in your professional capacity, might understand that biting and pinching are forms of communication, parents, especially those of the victim, often see this as an unacceptable and unprovoked attack on their child. The parents want the perpetrator 'dealt with' and the 'safety' of their own child ensured.

The way one approaches this with a parent whose child is actually doing the biting requires extreme diplomacy. The parent will feel shocked and may be ashamed, and could behave in rather a defensive manner. So what can the practitioner say? Reassuring comments need to be made:

- Your daughter is a lovely little girl and this biting is only a phase.
- She will grow out of it.
- We will monitor her behaviour so we can tell you what might be the triggers.
- We will tell you how she is getting on.
- We can give you some advice if you like.
- Maybe you can help us with this? How do you deal with this at home?

Sally's story

Sally owns and runs her own nursery and pre-school in a large rural village. The nursery has a family feel about it and most of the children come from the village. She wants to give the children a nurturing and stimulating environment and supports her staff well so there is an open dialogue with everyone.

Sally knew there was a little girl called Jessica who was biting other children and she had discussed with staff the strategies they could use to help Jessica. What she had not realised was that she had not explained clearly enough to her staff about 'how' to talk to Jessica's mother about this.

One day Sally overheard an inexperienced member of staff talking to Jessica's mother, when she came to pick her daughter up. The staff member was tired because it had been a difficult day with Jessica. However, Jessica's mother was also tired at the end of her working day. Sally was horrified because the first thing the mother was greeted with was, 'Oh, today has been a hard day for us. Jessica has been biting other children a lot.' Although this staff member had not meant to, she had upset Jessica's mother and Sally had to step in.

After this event, Sally spoke to her staff and explained that, however difficult a day they might have had with any of the children (whatever the issue), it is inappropriate to bombard a parent with negative comments the minute she walks through the door. She invited her staff to think about a better way to greet parents after a difficult session.

This is what they came up with and it can be a template for dealing with any behavioural problem:

- **Make a positive comment first** – 'We've had a lovely day; Jessica had some fun in the role play area.'
- **Tell about the problem** – 'Although Jessica has been lovely most of the time, there has been some challenging behaviour.' (More details can be given when the mother has had a chance to take this in.)
- **Ask the parent for help** – 'We'd like your advice about how you deal with this at home.'
- **Offer support** – 'Is there anything we could do to help you?'

Since this event, the member of staff has not only increased in confidence, she is more willing to ask Sally for support and has established a good working relationship with Jessica's mother.

The child who is ill

Babies and small children are regularly unwell. In fact, when children first start in nursery they usually pick up all the little bugs that are going around. The difficulty for the practitioner is what to do when you have a child who is delivered to your setting and is clearly unwell.

A typical scenario

A mother comes in first thing in the morning, Calpol in one hand, child in the other. She is in a rush to go to work. Her child does not look well but the mother says that he is just 'under the weather' and a 'bit of Calpol' will be all that he needs. The practitioner gets the form for the mother to sign. (The mother has forgotten that written permission has to be provided before staff are allowed to give a child any kind of medicine.) The mother leaves. Half an hour later the child is still pale and has a bit of a temperature. The practitioner is concerned, so she rings the mother, who tells her just to give him some Calpol now and he will soon be better. The practitioner gives the mother the benefit of the doubt and decides to keep an eye on the child, watching out for any rapid change to his condition.

Maybe this little boy will perk up. However, it is a difficult judgement to make when a parent is pressing the practitioner to keep the child. The parent may have work commitments and no extended family or friends to call on to help out. However, the child's interests have to come first and the welfare of the other children in the nursery has to be taken into account. If this child continues to look unwell, the practitioner will have to ask the parent to come and pick him up.

The unpleasant letter

It does not matter how many letter and cards you might receive that praise your work and express appreciation and delight, it is the 'unpleasant letter' that can be the one that is remembered and thought about and can cause terrible distress and undermine your confidence. Thorne (2003) described a nursery teacher as feeling 'all but annihilated' by a letter of complaint that had 'come out of the blue', because the father had 'always been charming and seemingly supportive and friendly'. I was recently told a similar story, and will tell it here, because it illustrates how a small misunderstanding can trigger a much more significant problem.

Norma's letter

This story is about a boy called Simon, who was four years old, and his mother Hilary. It is also about Norma, who was the manager of a privately run nursery. Simon only attended the nursery one day a week because he went to another nursery for the other four days. Hilary had wanted Simon to attend the other nursery full time, but they did not have a place, so Simon came to Norma's nursery. Hilary wanted to make sure that she had used her full free entitlement of nursery provision.

Simon settled in well and made a good relationship with his key person as well as the other staff. Hilary was very happy with Simon's placement and all went very well. There were no problems with this arrangement and it worked well for everyone.

It was getting near to the end of the summer term and Simon would soon be leaving for full-time school. There was to be a 'leavers' outing' at the seaside, but the scheduled day was not Simon's day at the nursery. Norma went to chat to Hilary one day and the outing cropped up in the conversation. Norma said she was sorry that Simon would be at the other nursery on the day of the outing. The conversation came to an amicable close and Norma thought no more about it.

However, the next morning a formally typed letter came in the post. Norma felt sick as she read all 680 words and had to sit down. Hilary said that she felt she had been treated very badly by the nursery and by Norma in particular. She accused Norma of saying that 'she didn't know Simon very well because he only came once a week so he wouldn't be missed at the outing'. Hilary then went on to say she was very offended and would be pulling Simon out of the nursery with immediate effect. She said she had been made to feel ostracised and accused Norma of being dismissive towards her and only interested in taking her fees.

Norma was devastated and wondered if she really had said these things and come across as dismissive. She showed the letter to some of her close colleagues and they were shocked. Norma was particularly attentive towards parents and the nursery was well known for its caring ethos. They told Norma that she

---

would never have said the things she was accused of and that Hilary had got the wrong end of the stick.

So Norma got on the phone straight away and arranged to meet Hilary, who came in later that day. Whilst some wounds were licked and things felt a little better, and Hilary apologised for her letter, she had still decided that Simon would leave the nursery early. However, Norma was able to negotiate a 'special last day' for Simon, so he did return for one more session and the very important ending for both Simon and the staff was able to happen.

The bigger picture

There was of course something behind that unprovoked outburst from Hilary and it was a pity that she could not have talked things through with Norma beforehand. Hilary had just heard that Simon had been refused a place at the school of her choice and was really distressed with the news. Somehow the reminder that Simon would not be at the outing felt like another rejection and Hilary expressed all her feelings of helpless frustration around the LEA decision in her letter to Norma.

The trouble with a letter is that it is 'permanent'. It is easier to forget a difficult conversation if the relationship is then repaired. However, if a letter is kept it will arouse those awful feelings every time it is reread.

Ofsted

As all settings, including the homes of childminders, are Ofsted regulated, there will be visits from Ofsted inspectors from time to time. Whilst this can be the opportunity to show an outsider the good quality of your provision, it usually brings high levels of anxiety about being 'judged'. Not only that, but the reports are read by both parents and prospective parents. The rating given in the report will influence whether or not a parent will choose to visit or select a place.

A recorded concern

I was told this story only very recently. Rory has been working in a nursery for about a year. He is well liked by everyone and thoroughly enjoys his work, bringing much life and enthusiasm in the nursery. However, one day one of the parents shared a 'small concern' with the manager, Stephanie. She said that her daughter, Emma, had told her some things about Rory that she felt 'unsure' about. Emma did not seem troubled and it had taken the mother about two weeks to get round to mentioning it.

Stephanie told the mother she would record it in her complaints/incidents folder and would look into it. It was thoroughly looked into but no one could find any substance to the story. Emma had a tendency to tell 'stories' and the mother acknowledged her daughter's vivid imagination. It was later established that the incident could not have occurred and the mother apologised to Rory. There was no harm done and the family and nursery staff did not think any more about it. They all considered the matter was closed. Rory continued his good work with the children and their parents.

Some time later the nursery had an Ofsted inspection. There were two inspectors, as one was supervising the other. Both of these people were very impressed with the nursery and it looked as if they were going to give a rating of 'outstanding'. However, when they took a look at the complaints/incidents folder the positive atmosphere changed.

'You know you have broken the law', said the inspector. Stephanie was horrified. 'It is an offence if you do not report an allegation.' Stephanie explained that what had happened was not a formal allegation but had been an expression of concern, the details of which were found to be untrue. She also explained that the mother had even apologised to the member of staff. All this had been written down.

The Ofsted inspector asked her superior what she thought. Her superior was uncertain, but the inspector was adamant the nursery had committed an offence and was going to take the matter further. The rating and report would have to wait. Three months later and the nursery is still awaiting its final report. The delay is because the difference between what is considered a concern and what an allegation is a grey area in the eyes of the law and no clear conclusion has been drawn. However, the problem seems to be about semantics and procedures rather than whether there was any professional misconduct. In the meantime, Emma's mother is horrified by what has happened and has written a formal letter to Ofsted. She explained that she had not made an allegation, but had expressed a minor concern that had been resolved. She also wrote that if there had been any doubt in her mind she would have withdrawn her child from the nursery immediately and would have got in touch with Ofsted herself.

This incident highlights the extreme sensitivity and lack of trust that is developing in our society about professional misconduct. It is important to be very clear about how you record any complaints or concerns so there is no ambiguity. At least in this particular nursery there are good channels of communication between the family and the staff and they are offering each other good support during this difficult time.

Special educational needs

The question of whether a child has special educational needs is another area which can create difficulties of communication between a practitioner and a child's parent. Special educational need is the formal term for any difficulties a child is experiencing, whether emotional, behavioural or developmental, that could be affecting his or her ability to learn. There are services that the nursery can call upon for advice. However, any concern should first be shared with a child's parents. This can be a difficult conversation. Most parents usually 'know' when something is not quite right, but would rather not notice in the hope that things will be okay. Some parents convince themselves so successfully that there is nothing wrong that it can come as a big shock to discover that anyone else might be concerned. Other parents genuinely may have no idea that their child is not developing in quite the same way as her peers.

A language problem

Thomas started at his nursery in the February, aged two years and nine months. He had been living and attending a nursery in France as his English parents are both ski instructors and had been working in the French Alps. Whilst the family spoke English in the home, the nursery was French-speaking and Thomas's parents were keen that Thomas should be bilingual. Thomas arrived in the English nursery unable to speak much English at all.

Caroline, the nursery practitioner, soon became concerned though. She had worked with speech and language therapists and speech disordered children in the past and it became apparent to her that there was something wrong with Thomas's speech. It was not just that he was 'delayed'. Many bilingual children are slower at both languages in the first three years but will catch up later and become fluent in both languages. Thomas, however, had poor speech patterns. He was making incorrect sounds and he struggled to make himself understood in either language. He was also not making the expected progress, despite Caroline's support.

Caroline knew that she would have to approach Rachel (Thomas's mother) about this, but she would need to be careful and tactful. She needed to be open and honest but at the same time sensitive and gentle. It is easy to come across as brutal when expressing concerns about someone else's child, because you can talk about the 'problem' in a way that can depersonalise the child.

This is how Caroline successfully talked with Rachel and is an example of how to approach and talk with parents about your concerns regarding their child's development. The timing of this conversation needs to wait until you have built up a trusting relationship with that parent.

- **Make positive observations first** – 'Thomas is a real darling; he has a great sense of humour and loves playing on the little slide.'
- **Be curious about the child at home** – 'Tell me something about what Thomas enjoys at home.'
- **Ask a 'Have you noticed . . .?' question** – 'Have you noticed that it can be a bit difficult to understand what Thomas is trying to say?'
- **Actively listen to the parent** – She might say, 'Yes! I have noticed this more since we have come back to the UK. I did wonder if he might have a problem.'
- **Acknowledge what the parent has said** – 'So you were wondering if he had a problem? I agree with you.'
- **Express concern but give hope** – 'Many children do have some difficulties with their speech when they start talking, and they soon grow out of it. We can do a lot to help, especially if we know more about it.'
- **Give the parent something to 'do'** – 'I would suggest you go and see your GP and request a hearing test.' (It is much easier for parents to take in this news if they can then do something practical.)
- **Listen to the parent's worries** – (At this point the parent usually brings out all her worries that she couldn't bear to express before.) 'I always knew there was something wrong but I didn't want to face up to it. Thomas is so little you see; I thought he would get better when he came to England. But since we have arrived I have noticed how the other children are really beginning to talk and Thomas can't say much at all. I blame myself for his problems; maybe we should never have carried on working in France. I try very hard to get him to say the words correctly but that seems to make things worse.'
- **Give reassurance and some practical guidance** – 'You have done nothing wrong and you are a lovely mum. Thomas is a happy and well-adjusted little boy. But he doesn't have to repeat things when he has said them wrong because that makes him a bit tense. All you need to do is repeat what he has said, so he hears it. It's called modelling and it really does help children.'

By the end of this conversation Rachel has been able to express and share her worries, realise she has some support, been reassured her son can be helped and been guided towards a practical next step that will help everyone (requesting a hearing test).

Whatever worries you or the parents may have about a child, it is really important that you can work on them together. It is worth having the 'difficult conversation'.

The responsibility of those working in the Early Years

Your work with families is of vital importance to the mental, emotional and physical well-being of our future generation. Do you realise just how important your work is? It needs to be acknowledged by you first. Not only do you need to acknowledge the importance of your work, you need to take responsibility for what you do and remember again, in your heart, why you went into this field of work in the first place. Caring for the education and welfare of young babies and children is not simply about 'minding' them whilst their parents do something else. 'Minding' is a demeaning word in such vital work, which is about cherishing, protecting and guiding other human beings. When you truly recognise and value the importance of your work, the parents will sense this and feel safer in entrusting their children to you.

Many parents bring their babies and tiny children to childcare settings because it is 'the thing we do' these days. The expectation of our government and society at large is for women to return to the workplace. We are told that nurseries will offer the very young a 'better start' if they have the stimulation of a nursery or pre-school experience. Whilst it is your responsibility to offer this 'better start', what about the parents themselves? How are they feeling? We have read, in Chapter 7, the terrible anxiety felt by a new mother as her little son Memhet found it difficult to settle. Your first and foremost responsibility to all babies, children and parents is to help them feel safe; help them feel they are being held in a safe pair of hands. Babies and children will not thrive or learn unless their parents feel that you really care. It is not about 'sounding professional'; it is about genuinely 'feeling' for that mother, who feels torn about separating from her beloved.

Many parents, especially those who have established a secure bond with their little one, feel very ambivalent about placing their child in childcare or pre-school. They feel they 'ought to' with their heads yet they feel 'torn apart' in their hearts. This makes the start of every placement, whether in a childminder's home or in a group setting, a difficult experience. We all know how nervous we feel when we start something new. Imagine that and then double it; well in fact more than double it. That is how parents feel in those early days when they bring their baby or child to you. If you are a parent yourself, you will probably recognise this feeling firsthand.

So let the main focus of your work be on helping new parents as well as their baby or child to settle in first. If you recognise that the quality of the relationships you have with the parents will affect the child's emotional and intellectual well-being, you will find yourself automatically making the effort to improve your own social skills so that the relationships are warm and genuine for all of you.

CHAPTER 10

Concluding thoughts: parents, practitioners and playfulness

Play and humour are present from the earliest months of life through the joyful interplay between a caregiver and a baby. The context for affectionate playfulness is found in the daily creation of small, ordinary opportunities for co-operative communication through loving face to face contact. This mutual pleasure derived from each other is a sign of well-being and a building block for sociability. Feeling good about ourselves in relation to others through shared laughter or anticipated rhythms of singing games, nursery rhymes and, later in life, family fun and shared humour for example, is about the stirrings of interest and pleasure in others. The earliest smiles, pre-verbal communication and sounds which are exchanged before words are the tools for adult communication as well. Such playfulness supports a willingness to give something a try with another and to see what happens next. When there is attuned communication and reciprocal interest, then curiosity is aroused about the intentions of another. What may hopefully be created together between two people is not only about what happens in the external space but also about subtle shifts of internal vitality that are created and actively sought by infants and adults alike.

Brain research is suggesting that when a baby sees her mother's smile this stimulates the release of 'feel-good' hormones which shape brain development. We know, too, that meeting flat, unmeaningful and negative expressions triggers the production of cortisol in babies' brains. Cortisol is a stress hormone which in turn blocks the production of feel-good hormones such as dopamine.

Smiles, therefore, provide quite literally a feel-good experience which releases feel-good biochemicals like dopamine and beta-endorphins. We know now that the development of the 'social' brain (located in the frontal cortex) is sculpted by such warm, positive communication. The discovery of the mirror neurone has revealed that simply observing another human being in action produces brain activity in an area of the brain as if the observer were involved in that action himself.

We might imagine how powerful being met by a smiling face at the threshold of the nursery really is for parents. If parents are met by preoccupied practitioners or teachers with a coolness of manner they will react and learn from that experience, whereas being acknowledged and affirmed by somebody who is in tune, responsive and consistent increases well-being. It is in the hands of staff to influence and improve these relationships. And these skills, happily, are within their reach as a result of their daily work with children.

Early Years practitioners often say that one of the contexts that helps to improve parent partnerships is 'Stay and Play' sessions. These special opportunities may be key to creating calm, loving environments where adults and children can flow together: reading, singing, sharing and cuddling together leaves all participants feeling held within a cherished community. Children often show an excited anticipation of 'Stay and Play', when their worlds inside and outside nursery quite literally come together. This shared attention, reciprocity and enjoyment of playing together with happy adults is an opportunity to strengthen a young child's sense of self. These occasions offer the chance for deep mutual satisfaction in an ever more competitive society. Groups of children and adults delighting in playing together offer 'islands of intimacy' (Goldschmied & Selleck 1996), which are quieter, kinder places that can be found throughout a lifetime when we need to draw from John Bowlby's 'internal pot of gold' laid down by many early experiences of deep security, warmth and love. Our emotional well-being and good mental health are rooted in these dynamic processes of play and good humour where we can flow.

It is every child's birthright to have moments of magic, wonder and spiritual nourishment which they themselves have asked for, and then to be 'served' by adults rather than to be in receipt of 'Services for Children'. Likewise, this book has attempted to make explicit how communication with parents serves to build relationships which are meaningful, respectful, clear and honest, and once this way of being between the adults has been established then the fun, enjoyment of shared activities and loving playfulness can really begin. The mutual surprise and delight found between adults in this way leads to a gift we give to children so they may become 'rich in potential, strong, powerful, competent and most of all, connected to adults and other children' (Malaguzzi 1997, p. 117 cited in Penn 1997).

Writing a book is close to the creative process of giving birth, and so it is always of interest to see who else has been born into the nursery of books! It is of great interest and joy to us as authors, therefore, that a recently published book that is passionate about the subject of childhood has burst onto the scene in such a timely manner. We will offer these final words from one contributor and join in the sentiment expressed:

'Children should not be required to ripen early. They should not be required to be what we think they should be, whether at home or at school. Parents and teachers can, and usually will, be the sowers of healthy developmental seeds in the early years; but the harvest must be left to the children' (House 2011).

We hope this book will help you sow the seeds of communication with your parents so you may stand back together and wonder at your children's growth and development.

Figure 10.1 *A father and a nursery practitioner laugh together, creating a triangle of love and trust for the small child, in an atmosphere of playfulness.*

Appendix: training workshop exercises

It may be helpful to use staff training sessions as an opportunity to practise some of the skills this book has introduced to you. Below are a series of exercises to get you started.

Individual exercises

Developing your sense of self through silent reflection

Working with young children is emotionally demanding work, and so making time to relax and recharge your vitality and find a space to prepare for a parent meeting is essential.

- Find a comfortable, quiet place where you will not be interrupted for a while.
- Relax and close your eyes.
- Imagine you are taking a five-minute holiday from work.
- Focus on your breathing: breathe in a long, deep breath and then breathe out a long deep breath.
- Imagine going to a favourite place outdoors that you love or the special place at home where you relax. See it in your mind's eye and enjoy being there.
- If any thoughts try to take your attention away from this scene, e.g. any tasks you have to do later, say in a gentle and relaxed way to these thoughts each time they come: 'I'm coming to you soon.' Let go of the thought.
- Notice what it feels like to be relaxed, and notice too the parts of your body you find it hard to relax.
- When you are ready, open your eyes, gently stretch and enjoy the calm clarity of thought you have given yourself in the middle of a busy day. Notice the way you feel before and after the exercise, before you return to your children or start the meeting.

Becoming a better communicator

At the start of each term, write down a personal challenge manifesto in relation to your communication skills; put it in your diary and review it before your next holiday break:

- One thing I would like to start doing is . . .
- One thing I would like to stop doing is . . .
- One thing I would like to continue doing is . . .

Developing your ability to notice

Find time each day before your children arrive to notice everything that is going on around you. Look at the activities you have set out, the objects in the room; notice any smells or sounds. Go to the window of your room and look out and notice the changes in nature and any seasonal changes. Do not evaluate what enters through your senses but just observe in preparation for the day ahead.

This exercise will help you develop your observational skills in relation to people too.

Pair work

Early experiences of communication in your family

- Who was the key communicator in your family?
- Choose three adjectives to describe what listening to that person communicating was like?
- How do you think this form of communication has influenced your communication skills?
- Whose communication skills do you admire and why? (It might be a family member, a friend or somebody in the media or in public life.)

What are your personal strengths and weaknesses when you are communicating with others?

Working independently at first, score yourself against the following statements in order of strength (6 = your best skill). Compare your assessments and share together with your partner how you might strengthen your weaker skills.

- I am good at drawing people out.
- I like to give information.
- I like to give advice and offer suggestions.
- I can be quite challenging in a conversation.
- I am at ease with other people who express their emotion when communicating.
- I am encouraging and validate the other person.

Developing communication in your setting

- What are the most successful forms of communication used in your setting?
- What are the areas of communication your setting needs to strengthen?
- What are the small steps and opportunities you can take to play a part in this change?

Developing effective listening and evaluating it

- One person talks to another for three minutes on any topic.
- The second person summarises what has been said from time to time.
- Roles are reversed and then both people comment on their experience of the activity.
- Each person comments on what she has liked or disliked about the exercise and how she will be able to carry across into her work what she has learned from the exercise.

Using open and closed questions effectively

- One person talks for three to five minutes about a new experience he has recently enjoyed.
- The other person asks six closed questions to gain further knowledge of the experience.
- Then the same person uses the open questions below to continue this exploration of the topic.
  I wonder if . . .?
  Could it be that . . .?
  What would happen if . . .?
  How would you respond to . . .?
  Do you think . . .?
  How would it feel if . . .?
- The two swap roles and at the end of the exercise they share with each other what they liked and disliked about the activity and how they will use what they have learned in their work with others.

Small group practice

What does it feel like not to be listened to? (three participants)

- One person attempts to engage another in conversation. (Describe your favourite film, book or holiday.)
- The second person shows in every way possible non-verbally that she is *not* listening.
- The third person observes and writes down all the non-verbal behaviour he has noticed.

Ask for feedback from the participant who has been ignored about what it felt like.

Decide on *one* thing you have learned from this exercise about body language and how you will use this new insight when you are communicating.

Is it ever worth pretending to understand when you don't?

- Give two of the three participants the opportunity to prepare a short dialogue using as much jargon and as many acronyms as they can think of, e.g. EYFS, PSED, CAF, etc.
- The observer is asked to describe the experience of listening to this conversation. (Although participants may understand some of the terminology, the aim of this exercise is light-hearted, at the same time as revealing what it might feel like for a parent to listen to such a conversation.)
- How difficult do you find it to stop somebody talking in this way and ask the meaning of things you do not understand?

Developing your paraphrasing, summarising and reflecting back skills

- One participant talks for five minutes on an important experience that shaped his choice of career.
- The second person listens and actively shows in her non-verbal body language that she is listening, and every so often she tries to paraphrase naturally what has been said without upsetting the rhythm of the conversation. At the end she offers a summary of the key points shared.
- An observer reflects back what he has observed.
- The other two participants share what has been helpful about the activity and what might have improved it.
- Swap roles and continue.

Group observation

Two participants are invited to role play being at a practitioner/teacher and parent meeting. They are problem solving together an emotive issue such as a child biting others or an accusation of bullying.

Facilitate a discussion using the following prompts

- What helps or hinders this encounter?
- What skills did you observe the practitioner/teacher using?
- What do you think each of the participants felt at the end of the meeting?
- How might this encounter have been improved?
- How appropriate and achievable are the targets that were set?
- Offer another pair an opportunity to role play some of the observing group's recommendations.

References and further reading

Ainsworth, M., Blehar, M., Waters, E. and Wall, S. (1978) *Patterns of Attachment: A Psychological Study of the Strange Situation*, Hillsdale, NJ: Lawrence Erlbaum Associates.

Baron-Cohen, Simon (2011) *Zero Degrees of Empathy: A New Theory of Human Cruelty*, London: Allen Lane.

Berne, Eric (1961) *Transactional Analysis in Psychotherapy*, New York: Grove Press.

— (1964) *Games People Play*, New York: Grove Press.

Bettelheim, Bruno (1987) *A Good Enough Parent*, London: Thames and Hudson.

Bowlby, J. (1969) *Attachment*, London: Pelican.

— (1988) *A Secure Base: Clinical Application of Attachment Theory*, London: Routledge.

Brazelton, T. Berry and Greenspan, S. (2000) *The Irreducible Needs of Children*, New York: Da Capo Press.

Bruce, T., Meggitt, C. and Grenier, J. (2010) *Childcare and Education*, 5th edition, London: Hodder Education.

Children's Workforce Development Council (2008) *Guidance to the Standards for the Award of Early Years Professional Status*, Leeds: CWDC (www.cwdcouncil.org.uk).

Cooper, G., Hoffman, K., Marvin, R. and Powell, B. (1998) *Circle of Security*, available online at http://www.circleofsecurity.org.

Decker, Bert (1989) *How to Communicate Effectively*, London: Kogan Page Ltd.

Department for Education and Skills (DfES) (2007a) *Every Parent Matters*, Nottingham: DfES Publications.

— (2007b) *Practice Guidance for the Early Years Foundation Stage*, Nottingham: DfES Publications.

— (2007c) *Social and Emotional Aspects of Learning (SEAL)*, Nottingham: DfES Publications.

— (2007d) *Statutory Framework for the Early Years Foundation Stage*, Nottingham: DfES Publications.

Directgov – Public services all in one place (2008) *Parental Rights and Responsibilities* (www.direct.gov.uk/en/Parents/ParentsRights/DG_4002954).

Dutton, K. (2010) *Flipnosis: The Art of Split-Second Persuasion*, London: Arrow Books.

Elfer, P., Goldschmied, E. and Selleck, D. (2011) *Key Persons in the Early Years: Building Relationships for Quality Provision in Early Years Settings and Primary Schools*, 2nd edition, London: David Fulton.

Fawcett, M. (2009) *Learning through Child Observation*, 2nd edition, London: Jessica Kingsley.

Fonargy, P. (2001) *Attachment and Psychoanalysis*, London: Karnac.

Gardner, Howard (1983; 1993) *Frames of Mind: The Theory of Multiple Intelligences*, New York: Basic Books (1983); London: Fontana Press (1993)

Gerhardt, Sue (2004) *Why Love Matters*, Hove: Brunner-Routledge.

— (2010) *The Selfish Society*, London: Simon & Schuster.

Goldschmied, E. and Jackson, S. (1994) *People Under Three: Young Children in Daycare*, London: Routledge.

Goldschmied, E. and Selleck, D. (1996) *Communication between Babies in their First Year*, video and booklet, National Children's Bureau, London.

Goleman, Daniel (1996) *Emotional Intelligence*, London: Bloomsbury.

— (1999) *Working with Emotional Intelligence*, London: Bloomsbury.

— (2006) *Social Intelligence: The New Science of Human Relationships*, London: Hutchinson.

Gordon, M. (2009) *Roots of Empathy: Changing the World Child by Child*, New York: The Experiment.

Harris, Thomas A. (1967) *I'm OK – You're OK*, New York: HarperCollins.

Harris, Thomas A. and Bjork, Amy (1986) *Staying OK*, London: Pan Books.

Hawkins, P. and Shohet, R. (2006) *Supervision in the Helping Professions*, Maidenhead: Open University Press.

Heaney, S. (1990) *The Cure of Troy: A Version of Sophocles' Philoctetes*, London: Faber.

House, Richard (2011) *Too Much, Too Soon? Early Learning and the Erosion of Childhood*, Gloucester: Hawthorn Press.

Howe, David, Brandon, Marian, Hinings, Diana and Schofield, Gillian (1999) *Attachment Theory, Child Maltreatment and Family Support: A Practice and Assessment Model*, London: Macmillan.

Kabat-Zinn, Myla and Jon (1997) *Everyday Blessings: The Inner Work of Mindful Parenting*, New York: Hyperion.

Kaplan, L. (1995) *No Voice Is Ever Wholly Lost*, New York: Simon & Schuster.

Karen, Robert (1998) *Becoming Attached*, Oxford: Oxford University Press.

Laevers, F. (ed.) (1994) *The Leuven Involvement Scale for Young Children*, Leuven: Centre for Experiential Education

Liedloff, Jean (1986) *The Continuum Concept*, London: Arkana.

Lindon, Jennie (2009) *Parents as Partners*, London: Practical Pre-School Books, A Division of MA Education.

Manning-Morton, J. and Thorp, M. (2003) *Key Times for Play: The First Three Years*, Maidenhead: McGraw Hill, Open University Press.

McCluskey, U. (2005) *To Be Met as a Person: The Dynamics of Attachment in Professional Encounters*, London: Karnac.

Mehrabian, Albert (1971) *Silent Messages: Implicit Communication of Emotions and Attitudes*, Belmont, CA: Wadsworth.

Minto, Arlo Wally (1994) *Communication and Understanding in Relationships*, Dallas: The Advisor Group.

Neil-Hall, J. (2007) 'Attachment: supporting young children's emotional well-being', *Optimus Early Years Update* 50.

O'Connell, B. (1998) *Solution Focused Therapy*, London: Sage.

Owen, Nick (2001) *The Magic of Metaphor*, Camarthan: Crown House Publishing.

Patterson, Kerry, Grenny, Joseph, McMillan, Ron and Switzler, Al (2002) *Crucial Conversations: Tools for Talking When the Stakes Are High*, London: McGraw-Hill.

Penn, H. (1997) *Comparing Nurseries: Children and Staff in Italy, Spain, and the UK*, London: Paul Chapman.

Read, Veronica (2009) *Developing Attachment in Early Years Settings: Nurturing Secure Relationships from Birth to Five Years*, London: David Fulton.

Rogers, C. (1951) *Client-Centred Therapy: Its Current Practice, Implications and Theory*, Boston: Houghton Mifflin.

Rozenthuler, Sarah (2012) *Life-Changing Conversations: 7 Strategies for Talking about What Matters Most*, London: Watkins Publishing.

Rustin, M. (1989) 'Encountering primitive anxieties', in L. Miller, M. Rustin and J. Shuttleworth (eds.), *Clearly Observed Infants*, London: Duckworth.

Schore, A. N. (2001) 'Effects of a secure attachment on right brain development, affect regulation and infant health', *Infant Mental Health Journal* 2.

Skinner, B. F. (1938) *The Behaviour of Organisms*, New York: Appleton Century Crofts.

Stern, D. (1991) *Diary of a Baby*, London: Fontana.

Stone, Douglas, Patton, Bruce and Heen, Sheila (2000) *Difficult Conversations*, London: Penguin.

Tannen, Deborah (1992) *That's Not What I Meant: How Conversational Style Makes or Breaks Your Relations with Others*, London: Virago.

Taylor Dyches, Tina, Carter, Nari J. and Prater, Mary Anne (2012) *A Teacher's Guide to Communicating with Parents: Practical Strategies for Developing Successful Relationships*, London: Pearson.

Thorne, Brian (2003) *Infinitely Beloved*, London: Darton, Longman and Todd.

Tolle, Eckhart (2003) *Stillness Speaks*, London: Hodder & Stoughton.

— (2005) *A New Earth*, London: Penguin.

Ward, Ute (2009) *Working with Parents in Early Years Settings*, Exeter: Learning Matters.

Whalley, M. and the Pen Green Centre Team (2008). *Involving Parents in their Children's Learning*, 2nd edition, London: Paul Chapman.

Wheatley, Margaret J. (2002) *Turning to One Another: Simple Conversations to Restore Hope to the Future*, San Francisco: Bennett–Koehler.

Williamson, Marianne (1996) *A Return to Love*, London: Thorsons.

Winnicott, D. W. (1964) *The Child, the Family and the Outside World*, London: Pelican.

— (1971) *Play and Reality*, London: Routledge.

— (1988) *Playing and Reality*, London: Pelican.

Wright, K. (1991) *Vision and Separation between Mother and Baby*, London: Free Association Books.

Zeldin, T. (1998) *Conversation: How Talk Can Change Your Life*, London: The Harvill Press.

Index